The Quest for the Creed

For Don Longenecker

"How good and pleasant it is for brothers to live together in unity." (Psalm 133:1)

The Quest for the Creed

*What the Apostles Really Believed and
Why it Matters*

by
Dwight Longenecker

A Crossroad Book
The Crossroad Publishing Company
New York

The Crossroad Publishing Company
www.CrossroadPublishing.com

© 2012 by Dwight Longenecker

Printed in the United States of America.
The text of this book is set in Venetian 301
The display face is Venetian 301

Project Management by
The Crossroad Publishing Company
We thank especially:
Editorial development: John Zmirak   Text design: Web Fusion
Cover design: Stefan Killen   Printing: Versa Press

Message development, text development, package, and market positioning
by The Crossroad Publishing Company

Books published by The Crossroad Publishing Company may be purchased
at special quantity discount rates for classes and institutional use. For
information, please e-mail info@CrossroadPublishing.com

Longenecker, Dwight.
The quest for the creed: What the Apostles Really Believed and Why it
Matters / by Dwight Longenecker.
       p. cm.
Previous edition published as: Adventures in orthodoxy. Manchester, N.H.:
Sophia Institute Press, c2003.
ISBN 978-0-8245-2674-0
1. Apostles' Creed. I. Longenecker, Dwight. Adventures in orthodoxy. II. Title.

BT993.3.L66 2013
238'.11--dc23

ISBN 13: 978-0-8245-2674-0

Table of Contents

Standing on My Head

THERE ARE SOME BRAVE revolutionary souls who stand on their head every day. They are not acrobats but artists, poets, mystics, comedians and prophets. Like children, they have a fresh way of seeing, and think it the most ordinary thing in the world to have a new idea, insight or enthusiasm. Furthermore, they think it most natural to share these epiphanies with others. It is their duty, their joy and their instinct to share their revolutionary insights, and they are always surprised when they are persecuted for their effort. If these acrobatic souls are like children, then there is one famous child who speaks for them all. He is the bright-eyed boy who appears in the story of the emperor's new clothes. Everyone in the court gasped with delight at the emperor's imaginary *haute couture*. Everyone in the crowd pretended to admire the emperor's invisible satin suit. Only the boy in the front row had the temerity to cry, "But he isn't wearing anything at all!" That child stands for every prophet, poet, artist, comedian and mystic in the world. He sees clearly what everybody else has been blind to, and declares with unembarrassed delight his joy at the emperor's nudity.

It is the boy's job to stand the world on its head, and in a world that is already convoluted, this means putting things the right way around. In other tales, the same task falls to the court jester. In Shakespeare's plays the jester is the one who speaks the hard truth to a character who has gone soft in the head. Sometimes the jester shocks and offends with blunt but clear statements. More often, he pops the balloon of pomposity with riddles and jokes, or puns and poems. Like the boy who laughed at the fat, naked emperor, the jester's job is to stand on his head and then make people see themselves and the world in a fresh way. For his labors the jester is always laughed at, but never thanked. In fact, he is more often persecuted for his efforts. His clients may laugh at the clown's red nose, but they will also tell him not to poke it into their affairs. If he pushes his prophecies and jokes too far the jester may be mocked, beaten, thrown into a well, or simply ignored.

This role attracts me. By nature I am one of those lugubrious optimists— liturgical on the outside, but anarchical on the inside. As the fool longs to play Hamlet, so this Hamlet has always longed to play the fool. I want to wear the jester's motley, dangle a little stick with a fool's head and a feather on the end, and wear rings on my fingers and bells on my toes. I want to scurry around in pointy slippers and poke my nose into our holy places—both the secular ones and the sacred ones. I want to enter the holy of holies and stand on my head so I can see it from a totally new perspective. If I can manage the gymnastics, then the floor may become the ceiling and the ceiling the floor. What seemed sacrosanct may turn out to be mundane, and what was mundane may burn with meaning.

I wish to stand on my head and see the world in a fresh way for two reasons. First of all, I get bored easily. I am sure this is a severe character fault, but I tire of seeing the world the same way all the time. This is the same reason I enjoy traveling, and why I once bought X-Ray vision glasses from the back of a comic book. The second reason I want to see the world in a fresh way is because it sometimes seems that the whole world is as mad as the crowd who oohed and aahed over the emperor's new clothes. If I can only catch a glimpse of the pink buttocks of reality I will not only be happy, but I might also get one or two others to enjoy the joke, and gasp with the freshness of everything.

One of the ways to do this is for us to see the whole thing with a fresh perspective. There are many ways to get a new perspective, but two ways work very well: laughter and anger. The reason jokes are funny is that they shock us with a surprising and subversive angle on reality. The things that make us angry also give us a fresh perspective. That's why we get angry: because some new event or bit of news has upset the comfy chair. So in this book I hope to juggle with the truth, tell a few jokes, do some back flips and stand on my head. Like most clowns, I expect I will annoy some people, and frighten others. If you turn up your nose at my style or content, then I will make you even madder by suggesting that I have hit my target. If you think I am too big for my britches, then imagine saying such a thing to a circus clown. He wears big britches on purpose. If you think I am a poseur, an impostor or simply a pompous ass, then I confess: You're right. But just remember that I am posing on purpose and playing the fool. I am strutting the stage as any jester does— knowing that true words are most often spoken in jest.

But have patience. Try to join in the spirit of the exercise. Don't be a party pooper, and most of all don't get me wrong. If I tickle you, it's because I want you to laugh, not cry. Some people assume the jester's hat because they are weary cynics who believe in nothing and mock everyone. Not I. I wear the jester's hat because I believe in all things and wish to mock no one. I am a cheerful, not a churlish jester. If I criticize people it's not because I believe they are bad the way they are, but because I think they can be better. If I suggest that people are hypocrites and fools, it is only because I am recognizing them as my brothers and sisters. If I shoot holes in peoples' pet theories, it is to remind us all that truth is leaky. So are people. I'm leaky. You're leaky. Everybody, like Liza's bucket, is riddled with holes, and it is only those who see how many holes they have who are holy.

This is the second edition of this book. It was first published under the title, *Adventures in Orthodoxy—The Marvels of the Christian Creed and the Audacity of Belief*. Unfortunately, the title confused people and they thought it was a book about Christians from Greece and Russia who like icons and baklava pastries and vodka and priests with long beards named Dmitri or Stephanopoulos. They were disappointed to find that it was a book by a Roman Catholic about the Apostle's Creed. To make matters worse, a clever editor illustrated the cover with someone who looked like Indiana Jones opening a church door. Like double knit leisure suits, it seemed a good idea at the time. The effect of this illustration was that those potential readers who did not think it was a book about Greek icons and Russian hermits imagined that it was a rip-roaring, page-turning adventure story. They too were sorely disappointed to discover that it was a book about theology, and immediately put the book on the shelf and never read it.

This is my favorite of all my books, but I am pessimistic that anyone else will enjoy it much because it is a religious book that two very common types of religious people will not like. The first kind of religious person I am thinking of is what we might call "ultra-orthodox." He is an inveterate dotter of I's and a crosser of T's. He likes bullet points and dogma and doctrine, and he prefers his religion like beef jerky—cut and dried and tough and pungent. The last thing it should be is challenging, funny, imaginative and edgy. Therefore, he will not like this book. The other sort of religious person I am thinking of is all concerned about "caring and sharing." For him, the faith is all about raindrops on roses and whiskers on kittens, and walking with Jesus on the beach and sometimes he carries you too. This sort of sentimental Christian likes creativity and warmth and "spirituality" well enough, but is not much on dogma and doctrine and orthodoxy and rubrics and rules and creeds and councils and canon law. I expect he will find any book on the creed "too rigid."

Therefore, if you are one of the rare sort of person who likes both orthodoxy and imagination, both dogma and delightful debate—if you are the sort for whom faith both should soar and be solidly grounded, then I think you might enjoy this book. I've tried to show how the Catholic religion is like flying a kite. The little paper diamond is you—picked up by a gust of wind and soaring into the clouds with imagination and delight, but you're bound to the ground with the twine of common sense and the good old, rock-solid, timeless Catholic faith.

Fr. Dwight Longenecker
Greenville, South Carolina
The Memorial of St. Joseph Cupertino, 2012

Losing Your Head

PICTURE A FAT, middle-aged Englishman trying to stand on his head. This is not just any Englishman. This is your honest-to-goodness Edwardian Englishman in a tweed suit. With his wide brimmed hat, a drooping mustache, walking stick and ridiculous pincenez, he looks like an overblown Teddy Roosevelt. The porcine face puffs as he tries to plant his head on the ground, then the chubby feet, stuck into stout boots, try to kick up into the air. The fat man kicks once or twice, wobbles, then on the third try he's up, feet waving and swaying for balance. His hat is squashed because he forgot to take it off. His tweed cape has fallen over his head. A button on his vest pops off with the exertion, then suddenly the pince-nez falls off and he instinctively reaches for it, loses his balance and comes crashing to the ground.

All of this to test the fat man's theory that "...it really is a fact that any scene, such as a landscape, can sometimes be more clearly and freshly seen if it is seen upside down."

The fat Englishman is named G.K. Chesterton, and he wrote those words about a skinny Italian called Francesco Bernardone, otherwise known as Francis of Assisi. Francis was a sort of holy acrobat, a wandering minstrel, a chevalier of the spirit—one of those fools who not only see the world upside down, but turn the world upside down. In his fat English way, Chesterton was a similar sort of clown, and his observation that the world is often more clearly seen upside down is revolutionary.

It's revolutionary not because Chesterton is a jolly English Che Guevara, but because, when you stand on your head you *revolve*. Revolutions upset the status quo by challenging the majority view. This kind of rebellion is both frightening and admirable. (Witness our feelings towards any adolescent with a safety pin in his eyebrow, a surly expression and purple hair.) The sort of revolution Chesterton advocates is subversive toward both sides— like a court jester who cracks jokes to those who are solemn, and assumes a funereal face for the frivolous.

For our lives to achieve their full potential, each one of us must go through a revolution. That is, we must learn to see things in a startling and fresh way. Such revolutions are exciting, but risky. There is much to gain, but much to lose. Therefore, being cautious as cats, we usually choose to stay right side up and do everything we can to avoid a revolution. In this way even the most nonconformist of us are unbearably respectable. Although we realize this truth, we still resist anything that might turn our world upside down. We prefer to plod on in our old habits and prejudices, because to launch out into something new is simply too frightening. We are like the seven-year-old who longs to ride the roller coaster, but can't work up the nerve.

Sometimes the necessary revolution in life happens through education, sometimes it happens through religion, but more often it comes to us as the result of some wonderful or disastrous event in life. We get a promotion or we get cancer. We hit the jackpot or we hit rock bottom. We fall in love or we fall off a ladder. Whether it comes through joy or sorrow, we have a sudden stupendous vision that turns our world upside down. Some people pursue this sudden insight and embark on a quest for meaning. They learn to hunger for those daily revelations that amount to daily revolutions. Most of us, however, get a brief glimpse of the Promised Land, then relapse into our usual cautious selves, forever wary of that dangerous revolutionary who lurks within, and who, for one delicious and dangerous moment, peeped over the parapet. We worry about that fellow, and sensing that the way of revolution is the way to lose everything, we step back to safety.

But sometimes there is more to be lost by not being a revolutionary. This is true for societies as well as individuals. Madame Guillotine reminds us that the time comes when those aristocrats who refuse to stand on their heads will lose them. Therefore, although there is a clear risk in revolution, there may be a greater risk in resisting it. We think it would be terrible to change the way we are; then one day the truth dawns that it would be even worse just to stay as we are. Suddenly Socrates' words, "The unexamined life is not worth living," hit us like a punch to the solar plexus. At that point, standing on one's head suddenly seems attractive, and sometimes we have just the jolt we need first to examine our lives, and then to re-make them. If we reach this point, our whole lives might start to spiral upward rather than flow down the drain.

Personal revolutions can happen in any area of life. We may suddenly see our job, our marriage, or our waistline in a truthful way for the first time. There are some ar-eas in our lives, however, where it is most difficult to see things freshly. These are the sacred places of our beliefs. Like ancient temples, these sanctuaries are built in stone, and like all holy places, they are inviolable. On their walls are carved the arcane symbols and sacred tenets of the faith that must never be questioned, even if it is not un-derstood. Religious people acknowledge that they have such sacred spaces in their lives. What is often misunder-stood is that non-religious people also have holy places where no blasphemy or heresy is allowed.

Everyone has some sort of belief system. In other words, we have a pattern in our mind that enables us to make sense of the world. We *believe* in this pattern, for by it we understand everything else. The pattern may be distorted and untrue. It may be conscious or unconscious, but it is there, as sure as our heartbeat. Our beliefs may be developed into a complex and beautiful system of religious dogma and devotion, or they may simply be the inchoate set of assumptions we have received from our parents, peers, teachers and the advertising industry. We may not be conscious of our beliefs—indeed we may deny that we have any—but even the denial itself is a kind of belief. In fact, it is arguable that unconscious beliefs exert a far stronger hold on us than the conscious ones. So, for example, we might consciously doubt the infallibility of a pope's decisions, but we would never think to doubt our own. So all of us have sacred spaces. We all have beliefs, and we instinctively protect and defend those beliefs against every kind of revolutionary threat.

Now, what troubles me about these sacred spaces is that most often they are *comfortable*. They are furnished with recliner chairs, whose most famous brand is called the La-Z-Boy. I am suspicious of any belief system that makes the believer comfortable, because it is probably the construction of a lazy boy. I speak here from experience because I realize how lazy I am and how much I love my own comfort. I am aware how easily I believe things which may be ridiculous or dangerous, simply because they make me feel better. Of course, a comfortable belief may be true, but if you think for a moment, isn't a belief that makes the believer uncomfortable more likely to be true? An uncomfortable belief is more likely to be true because we wish it weren't true. And if we wish something weren't true, it is less likely that we have made it up. This brings me back to the reason for a revolution. If we want to find out what is true, then we have to get out of the recliner chair and do some gymnastics. We have to stand on our heads and see the world in a fresh way.

This means we must not only acknowledge that we have beliefs, but we must find out what they are. This exercise is like lifting up a log and finding a world of living things underneath. Some of our discoveries will be delightful, and some disgusting. Once we find our beliefs, we must poke them to see if they are alive, rather like a boy pokes a dead snake...just to make sure. Just like that boy, we have to poke our beliefs to see whether they are true or not. This requires some thinking, and that sounds like a boring chore. But why do we consider thinking to be a boring chore? Probably because we have been taught to use thinking to solve problems and answer questions. But what if we were to turn that around and use thinking not so much to solve problems, but to create them, and not so much answer questions, but to pose them? Then thinking begins to undermine the dull establishment rather than support it.

To my mind this is the essential task of religion and education, yet most religions and schools do exactly the opposite. Rather than posing the questions, they furnish the answers. Instead of creating problems, they promote ready-made solutions. In fact, they actually oppose people who ask awkward questions. That is one of the reasons that the religious teachers killed Jesus and Socrates. This institutional suppression of honest questions is the reason so many people have no time for formal religion or education. They are curious and intelligent, and would rather work on a puzzle than peek at the answer page.

By standing on our head, we pose fresh questions, because we have looked at things in a fresh way. This questioning, however, is not the same thing as total skepticism. We stand on our head because we are enthusiastic and inquisitive. We ask questions because we want answers. Skepticism, on the other hand, asks questions because it doesn't believe there are answers, and creates problems because it likes to be destructive. It is the difference between the messy studio of an artist and the messy street of an anarchist.

There are two types of belief systems that are comfortable, and therefore require a fresh perspective. One type says there are no answers, and the other says that it has them all. The first of these belief systems is very common in our society. It goes by many names, but it can be called cynical nihilism. Nihilism is that belief which believes nothing, and cynicism is that belief's accompanying emotion. Cynical nihilism holds that there is no real meaning to the universe, or if there is, it can't be known. This bleak belief has been around since the Stoics, and is very commonplace. Although it sounds cruel to the point of despair, cynical nihilism is held by a great many people who are otherwise quite cheerful, and this leads me to suspect that cynical nihilism is not actually a cruel belief, but a comfortable one. And when I stand on my head, I can see this is true, for if there is no real meaning to the universe, then there is no real meaning to what I do. I may therefore do what I like, and this is a very comfortable belief indeed.

The other, and far more noble reason to embrace nihilism is that a person has lived through some mindless terror, and cannot see any meaning within the blind torture and suffering of millions. It is understandable that the torture and slaughter of the innocents provokes a nihilistic rage, but the emotions of rage and ultimate despair assume that there must be some meaning somewhere—even if it seems impossible to discover; otherwise the rage and despair would themselves be meaningless wasted energy.

But most nihilists are not so conscious as that about the emptiness of their belief system. Many people believe there is no ultimate meaning to the universe, but they do not express their belief. Their doubt that the universe has meaning is buried under the many layers of ordinary daily life. They never give it much thought, so they never express their belief. Their belief is expressed for them by one of their famous archbishops, the biologist Professor Richard Dawkins. So he states the creed clearly when he writes, "the universe we observe has precisely the properties we should expect if there is at bottom no design, no purpose, no evil, no good, nothing but pointless indifference."

This statement sounds grand in a theatrical and tragic sort of way. But have you seen the joke? If it is true that there is no purpose to the universe, we have to ask why Professor Dawkins writes books on purpose. In other words, if the universe is random and meaningless how can we write books that are planned and meaningful? Can the universe really be meaningless? If it were, the statement "the universe has no meaning" would itself be meaningless. To put it simply: the only thing that really is meaningless is the statement that all things are meaningless. If it is true that there is no meaning, then the whole solemn system that proclaims that there is no meaning itself has no meaning. It is a spectacle of sound and fury, signifying nothing. To put it the other way around, if the statement, "the universe has no meaning" is true, then the universe must have meaning.

By standing on our heads, we are able to see that cynical nihilism is only a solemn charade, but that is not the same thing as attacking it. In fact, it is impossible to attack cynical nihilism with serious argument, for how can you attack an emptiness? How can you reason against a belief that says reason is impossible? Can you negate a consistent negation? Can you attack a vacuum or lead a gallant charge against a ghost? Of course not. Solemnity can only be undermined with hilarity. A denial can only be attacked with an affirmation. Cynical nihilism must be countered not by argument, but by action. Like the hippie who put a flower in the soldier's gun, we must place into the void of modern thought something fresh and alarming. We must make a statement that is at once hilarious and annoying

If we are locked into the sad belief that there is no meaning in the universe we need to see the universe from a fresh perspective. In place of the dead-end despair of cynical nihilism, we need to catch a glimpse of a bizarre and beautiful open-ended universe—a universe where anything can happen, and life is a constant struggle between mystery and meaning, chaos and design, purpose and free will. The antidote to empty meaninglessness is an unembarrassed and rambunctious, full-blooded kind of belief. Instead of a universe with no meaning, we choose a universe where meaning surges forth from every molecule and star. This kind of belief is not taught but *caught*. It spreads like laughter at a circus or tears at a tragedy, for it is a trait far closer to both laughter and tears than rituals and rules. Such belief is not mere, mindless adherence to a dull dogma, but the terrible, tender contemplation of an incomprehensible mystery.

The second belief system that needs to be seen afresh is formal religion. In the face of cynical nihilism, the religious people come forward wringing their hands. They have always been a bit embarrassed by the public irrelevance of their beliefs, and now it seems society has called their bluff. Their response has been to sugar the pill of religion. Some religious entrepreneurs have replied by turning the ancient and mysterious faith into a game show. Their churches are full of people desperate to play "Who Wants to Be a Spiritual Millionaire?" The more tasteful religious executives have efficiently excised the awkward bits like the angry God, miracles and eternal damnation, and kept the nice bits like angels, being good and making the world a better place. In doing so, they have watered down the wine and tamed the lion. They have taken a religion worth dying for, and made it not worth getting out of bed for. Still others have retreated from the game shows and tea parties into an underground network of sour, legalistic reactionaries who can do nothing but wag their finger and splutter incoherent imprecations against the wicked world. Then they wonder why people don't go to church.

Many people (including many who go to church) view religious belief as impossible, irrelevant and absurd, but they never stop to consider that it is the impossible which often happens, the irrelevant which turns out to be most necessary, and the absurd which unlocks true meaning. After all, it was one of the world's first theologians who came up with the delightfully anarchic statement, "You ask how I can believe the absurd? Because it is absurd I believe." No one wants a religion that is easy to believe any more than they want the ascent of Everest to be accomplished by helicopter. Religion, like mountain climbing, is meant to be difficult. For religion to have a cutting edge it has to actually glory in its seeming impossibility, its apparent irrelevance and monstrous absurdity. One mustn't mistake this seeming absurdity for empty meaninglessness. The ancient theologian's absurdity is a riddle with an answer—in contrast to nihilism, whose only answer is that there is none.

This is the sort of belief I wish to embrace—a belief that is tough, bracing and revolutionary, a belief that turns our whole world upside down. To encourage this revolutionary way of seeing, this book will reflect on the words of the Christian creed. This is not because this is the most respectable way to expose the nakedness of modern thought, but because it is the most embarrassing, blatant and ridiculous way. What could be more of a scandal in a mechanical, scientific society than to propose a formula of supernatural dogmas? What could be more certain to set a stink bomb in the dinner party than to suggest such an outrageously outmoded proposition as a *creed*? But this is precisely what I propose. In the face of a society which is novel, subjective and uncertain, I offer the creed because it is ancient, objective and sure. I propose the creed because it is solid and substantial, not fluid or ephemeral. Like the philosopher who kicked the rock to prove that matter exists, I will kick the stumbling block of the creed, and then hop about holding my foot. Furthermore, the creed is practical and ordinary, not esoteric and exotic. It is both reactionary and revolutionary, out of date and up to date. The creed is meat and potatoes, not milk and water. It is something you can bite into and debate, something you can love and hate.

While I propose a creed, I am the first to admit that the creed, on its own, is not enough. You might as well say a ladder is good enough to climb to the moon. Those who wish to limit the spiritual quest to doctrinal statements are just another type of dull accountant. The solemn nihilists of our age may need a whoopee cushion under their seat, but the po-faced religionists of our age also need to wake up. Perhaps the creed can be used like one of those churchwarden's wands with a feather on one end and a knob on the other. If the warden cannot tickle them awake, then they get a knock on the head. With any luck, the very creed the dull religionists have turned into a certificate of religious correctness might be used to wake them up.

Do not imagine that I want you to believe the creed. At least, I do not want you to believe the creed in that dull way expected by generations of starchy and well-intentioned catechists. Their kind of belief in the creed is like belief in a dinner menu, a business contract or a toaster warranty. That kind of belief is simple acceptance of a necessary list on the basis of authority. Forget it. It may be better to disbelieve the creed than to believe in the creed on those terms. That kind of dull religion has inoculated millions against the sort of vital belief that revolutionizes the world. They've signed up for the creed thinking it was the end of the story, when it is only the table of contents. Religion is not a checklist of rules and beliefs. Its first job is not to give us all the right answers, but to pose the proper questions. Religion's whole point is to constantly make us stand on our head, to bring us to the brink of that great chasm called mystery and allow us to teeter there on the edge of the blazing darkness.

The purpose of all the ritual and rigmarole is to take us beyond the exercise and into the unexpected.

The seemingly dull creed turns every type of pedestrian orthodoxy on its head. It does so because the creed bursts with magnificent meaning. It explodes with unexpected and eternal insights. It is a concise cathedral, seemingly small but crammed with hidden nooks and corners that harbor endless nuances of light and shadow. The creed teases with everlasting contradictions and paradoxical possibilities. The creed is not the final definition of belief, but a springboard from which to discover the ancient, ever-youthful truth. It provides a fixed point, a starting block to run the race. I hope these reflections will show that the creed does not narrow things down but opens things up; it does not limit my mind, it expands my mind. The creed is not a chair but a ladder; it is a trampoline, not a mattress. Contemplating the creed turns the whole world upside-down. Therefore, if it is doing its work properly, the creed upsets the comfortable atheist and the sleepy believer alike.

Finally, I propose the creed because it is the language of the layman. These are the words that millions of ordinary people have said in church for thousands of years. I am not a professional theologian, philosopher, artist or academic. I speak instead for the man in the street. If you are standing in the crowd watching the flamboyant circus parade of life, then I hope you will enjoy this book. I hope it enrages you, delights you and moves you so much that it will make you think. If it does any of this, then I have done my job, juggled a few thoughts in the air, told some jokes and then bowed out so the real drama of belief and faith and life can begin.

CHAPTER ONE

The Man from Missouri

I Believe...

WHAT MAKES ME glum is that so many people who say they believe don't believe enough to take a risk. What do they believe in? They "believe" in their country, their political party, their religion, their way of life. "Belief" has become a boundary to life rather than a way to bound into life. "Belief" has become a fortress, a bolt hole, a comfort zone, an easy chair. They think they believe in a religion. What they really believe in is their own security.

Even worse, for the religious person "belief" means taking refuge in a list of intellectually understood theological propositions. It means ducking down and hiding within a belief system which they secretly suspect is a load of bunkum, but which they do not have the courage to challenge. These cowards subscribe to the "belief," because to doubt it would be a step into the dark and an adventure into the unknown. So they cling to their religion as a security blanket to ward off the attack of the secular zombies they fear so much.

Belief is not a dull adherence to a set of theological propositions, nor is it a robotic obedience to a set of moral principles. Belief is not the reason to stay at home. It's the reason to leave home and set out on the great adventure. Because "belief" has so often become a stale and timid imitation of life, people with backbone have dismissed belief as a security blanket for thumb-sucking losers. They have taken the option of cynicism, doubt and sarcasm, or imagined themselves brave by declaring themselves agnostics or atheists.

True belief is something else, and this book aims to jolt you out of your little Kansas farmhouse, swoop you up into the whirlwind and sweep you off to a Technicolor land where things are not what you expected. So fasten your seat belt, Dorothy. Watch out for the white rabbit, Alice, and prepare for a new view of yourself, your religion, your world, your everything.

Dorothy's dull Kansas is next door to dull Missouri. As Dorothy fled Kansas, so my entire life has been a persistent attempt to run as far from Missouri as possible. Yet wherever I turn, I find myself living in Missouri anyway. Missouri, as any home-grown American will tell you, is the "Show Me" state, because the man from Missouri won't believe it unless he sees it. This mythical Missouri man is the archetypal squinting, chin-rubbing yokel who won't be taken in by nobody, no way, no how. If Missouri is a flat state in the middle of America, it stands in for a flat state of mind in the middle of our culture. Sadly, Missouri man is everywhere now and he is not only a local yokel. He can be found at every level of society, from the street cleaner to the sophisticate. A cynical and suspicious attitude has found its way into our society and irritates, not like a pebble in a shoe, but like a gaping hole in a sole. In other words, it irritates as an absence, not a presence. As a result of this empty space, no one is to be trusted. No one has the answers. Nothing can be believed.

There is nothing wrong with healthy skepticism. It makes for a jolly pastime. It unmasks the charlatan, defrocks the fraud, suspects the superstitious and hoots at the hypocrite. Healthy skepticism takes potshots at all forms of pomposity and pretense. Have you noticed how children are healthily skeptical? When they watch the mayor strut by in his cockaded hat or the bishop glide in looking like an upholstery exhibit, they may be amused, but they are not impressed. A child is skeptical because he is curious, and he is curious because, at heart, he is a believer. In his discovery of the world, the child believes truth is possible to discover, and so he healthily sniffs out anything that masks or distorts the truth.

Unhealthy skepticism, on the other hand, is sour and suspicious. Unhealthy skepticism doesn't actually believe there is such a thing as truth. One needn't be a radical nihilist to disbelieve in truth. It is enough, like the urbane theologian, to smile weakly through the sherry and say, "What works for you is true for you." What the theologian is really saying is that all truths are of the same value, but this is another way of saying that truth is of no value, for how can all things be equally true? Can blue be orange, depending on your point of view? Can a dose of arsenic "work for me" and "not work for you"? Can two plus two equal seven if you simply alter your perspective? Can philosophy be reduced to a shrug of the shoulders and, "You say tom*a*to and I say tom*ah*to?"

Another form of polite nihilism denies the possibility of truth by asserting that what is true is the same as what is attractive. Truth is attractive, but the advertising industry teaches us that what is attractive is not always true. Another clever way to deny that there is such a thing as truth is to say that truth changes from one age or culture to another. Certainly the expression and emphasis of truth takes different forms at different times and in different cultures, but that does not mean the truth changes. An American may call it turquoise, an Englishman may call it aquamarine. They may argue whether they are referring to a color or a gemstone, but to both, bluish green is still bluish green. All of these are polite and clever forms of denying the possibility of truth, but behind the clever repartee lurks the chin-rubbing hayseed from Missouri who doesn't believe in truth at all.

Part of the problem is that the man from Missouri suffers from a "merely mechanical mentality." For him, facts are the only truth, and the only certain thing is that which can be explained. By explaining how a mysterious thing works, the man from Missouri believes he has explained the mystery away. But there is a problem with this, isn't there? Have you ever noticed how the more we probe into a mystery, the more mysterious it becomes? It seems that every answer only produces another question. Whenever we discover how something in the natural world works, there seems to be another factor left to explore. Doesn't this lead to the conclusion that everything is more than what it is made of, and more than the way it works? If so, then it is a strange truth that the very act of trying to explain the mechanics of a mystery only pushes us further into the unknown—and if it pushes us further into the unknown, then it hasn't solved the mystery, but compounded it.

At this point one has to admire the tenacity of the man from Missouri. When faced with a mystery that made our ancestors wonder and worship, the Missourian pushes back his ball cap, scratches his head, and says, "Aw shucks, there must be some other explanation." And he proceeds to poke and prod and cook up another theory. This laudable tenacity has helped produce all the great inventions and technological steps forward, but what is lacking in our hero's approach is any sense of wonder—that instinctual awareness or lurking suspicion that there might be more to life than flywheels and cogs and chemical reactions. Where did such a prosaic mindset come from?

It is easy to blame that hard-bitten old Dame Science, who taught us that we should only trust what we discover ourselves. It is true that science can be cynical, but bright science is open, inquisitive and unafraid of the unexplainable. Science is not the problem, and it is often part of the solution. Professor Dawkins is right when he says good science is both poetic and passionate for truth. Blaming our present lack of belief on science is too easy, because there are plenty of believing scientists and many more unbelievers who are not scientists. We may study the development and decay of philosophy or pin the blame on sociology, psychology, Marxism, capitalism, Darwinism or any other "ism" or "ology," but our pin will have missed the point. Unbelief may have used all the "isms" and "ologies" but the disease of unbelief is deeper and older than they all are. Unbelief is not particularly modern. The ancestry of Missouri man can be traced back to the very beginning of mankind's struggle. Missouri man is as ancient as Cro-Magnon man. There have always been human beings who have found it impossible to believe.

Since the days of our ancestor, Cain, we have found it difficult to believe because we have found it difficult to obey. Belief is never simply an intellectual exercise. As rational beings with bodies as well as brains, we cannot acknowledge something as true without also admitting that, if so, it must change our life. If something is true—really, utterly and radiantly true—why then it demands our total allegiance. If something is eternally and magnificently true, then it was here before I was and it must change me—I cannot change it. If the source of truth has given commandments that are true, then our complete and courageous obedience is required. No matter who the person is, or in what age they have lived, belief that demands obedience is, and always will be, a terrifying and exhilarating prospect.

The mere word "obedience" is a shock to the heart. It is enough to make you throw a book across the room. Obedience? Immediately images of mindless military obedience spring to mind. We see hoards of jackbooted thugs goose-stepping to the commands of their demonic overlords. The word "obedience" makes us think of purse-lipped old nuns ready to thrash timid children into submission. We imagine gullible religious devotees submitting to bizarre beliefs. We think of the young automatons of religious sects and the quivering woman shielding her children from the demands of an outrageous husband. All of these are not obedience but domination and subservience. The obedience that goes with belief is something different. It is an inquisitive, youthful, and open-ended virtue. After all, the root of the word "obedience" means "to listen," and what is true belief if not an open-hearted listening to the mystery at the heart of things? True obedience is a kind of curiosity. It is a fresh alertness, a child-like eagerness to listen and learn. It is the voice of deep calling to deep. It is a human heart open to the drawing and calling of a timeless and universal power which the ancients could only call Love.

This is the terrible beauty that lies at the heart of the quest that is faith, but the religious people's supper club has too often replaced that volcanic heart of fire with a plaster statue (perhaps of the Sacred Heart). I do not say this because I am a sculpture snob, but because the plaster statue of Jesus with his heart on the outside is a dusty and dead image, not a living force. This is why I enjoy it when statues actually begin to bleed. Now that is much more like real religion. That stands the world on its head. That is the sort of wild thing that makes my heart sing. When such a subversive event takes place, I begin to believe that my own tacky, plaster heart might also one day start to be alive again. At that point I remember that the universe is alive in more ways than I can imagine, and that there really is more to religion than bad hymns, banalities, and bingo.

To say "I believe" is more than belonging to a suburban special interest group which raises funds for charity. To believe is more than forcing ourselves to suspend our incredulity long enough to accept a few archaic metaphysical propositions. It is more than playing a spiritual lottery game that offers goodies rather than demanding goodness. In the most ancient creed, we say with magnificent simplicity, "I believe... in all things visible and invisible." At this point nothing is demanded but an open mind and open heart and a certain insouciant dignity. This is the first step: to develop a state of mind that accepts rather than rejects, that sees possibilities, not problems, that is instinctively inquisitive, not cynical, and sees meaning rather than absurdity. The first step is not to believe all the specifics, but simply to Believe. To Be. To Live. To Be Alive. To Believe.

To believe in all things visible and invisible is to accept the whole realm of all that is natural and supernatural. It means embracing, as one's own, every morsel of matter— from each grain of sand to each gargantuan star. It means being full of wonder at all things invisible, from atoms, memes and miracles to angels, molecules and monsters. It means accepting that the visible and invisible realms are intermingled in marvel and mystery. It means gasping with delight at the wonderful and frightening realization that *all things are possible*. This is the innocent, unembarrassed and blessed state of the believer: His heart is open to everything on earth and heaven, and he plunges in to be overwhelmed by it all, crying, "I believe!"

The romantic pastor Schleiermacher put it in terms philosophical. To believe is "to accept everything individual as a part of the whole and everything limited as a representation of the infinite." Dostoevsky's tender monk Alyosha knew what it meant to believe in all things visible and invisible. After the death of his friend Zossima, he stumbles outside and is touched by the interconnection of earth and heaven.

The vault of heaven, full of soft shining stars, stretched vast and fathomless above him....The gorgeous autumn flowers, in the beds around the house were slumbering till morning. The silence of earth seemed to melt into the silence of the heavens. The mystery of earth was one with the mystery of the stars. Alyosha stood, gazed, and suddenly threw himself down on the earth. He did not know why he embraced it. He could not have told why he longed so irresistibly to kiss it, to kiss it all. But he kissed it weeping, sobbing and watering it with his tears and vowed passionately to love it, to love it forever and ever....But with every instant he felt clearly, as it were tangibly, that something firm and unshakable as that vault of heaven had entered into his soul.[1]

How can the bland despair of the man from Missouri compare to such exquisite passion? How can the everlasting boredom of the nihilist compare to such a vibrant life? How can the yawn-inducing rituals of most religions compare to this heart-rending vision of reality? In response to "I believe... in all things visible and invisible," the man from Missouri can only shrug his shoulders and say, "I believe in nothing." As a result, the poor man has nothing, and he may ultimately become nothing. The timid religionist will also run from this vision of reality

---

[1] *The Brothers Karamazov*, Tr. Constance Garnett. New York, Random House, 1950, p. 436

to take refuge in his dogma kennel. He does so because this kind of belief is bigger than all theological propositions and threatens those boundaries he was using for security. Oblivious to their fears, the believer cries with open arms, "I believe...in all things visible and invisible!" and in saying so, like Alyosha, he possesses all things and will one day become one with that One in whom all things consist.

Still we draw back, afraid at what we might lose, but never seeing what we may gain. We are more frightened of the glory we do not know than the misery we know. Belief stands and beckons like a magnificent and majestic cherubim, but still the man from Missouri whispers in our mind that we might be fooled. We might be taken in. There is certainly proper cause for caution. The true believer is not gullible. He is healthily skeptical of charlatans, frauds, mind games and tricks—especially of the kind he is likely to play on himself. If we wish to believe, there is the danger of being gulled—but even if we are fooled and taken in, is there anything so very terrible in that? If it is all a huge cosmic joke, isn't it better to share in a joke, than not to laugh, or never to have heard the joke at all? If belief is an absurd mistake and there is not a Judgment Day, then nothing has been lost; but if there is a Judgment Day it will be far better to have believed too much than not to have believed enough. Even in this life, which is better—believing in all things visible and invisible, or believing in nothing? Choose you this day whom you will serve—all things radiant in earth and heaven, or the dark silence of empty space. Will you believe and choose delight, or not believe and choose despair?

Of course, to believe in all things visible and invisible requires a risk. The man from Missouri is a belt-and-braces man. He carries double insurance. He bolts and locks the door, and never takes a risk. The true believer, on the other hand, is forever taking risks. He knows the only sign of being alive is change. He takes the leap of faith. He jumps from the trapeze stand into the void, believing that the partner's arms are there.

Still the voice of fear whispers in our hearts, warning that such extravagant belief will demand something from us. We might be led down a trail that demands "not less than everything." We may have to face even death itself. Is this a reason or an excuse? We are going to face death anyway. In any case, no one is pretending that sacrifice is not part of the bargain. There is no small print in the creed. The One who calls makes it clear that your fears are justified. Indeed, everything will be required. Not one shred of doubt, cynicism, unbelief and fear may remain. Not a scrap of false pride, bigotry, narrow-mindedness, jealousy or rage will be allowed to stay. Not one morsel of squalid lust, envy or bitter resentment will be permitted to rot and fester in your heart. All of it must go, and it will not go without a kind of burning torment. It is true that the way of belief requires both ecstasy and agony. To love requires the hatred of all that is not love. Joy can never be real without sorrow, and new life is only available to those who are willing to die.

So first of all I say, "I believe." I state it with defiance and fear. With defiance in the face of a world where the man from Missouri seems to be winning. With fear because the act of belief forces me to consider the alternatives. If I, and others like me, are the only force in the universe then I and my friends are terribly alone and life has no final meaning. So with defiance and fear, like the primitive tribesman who stares at the stars and trembles, I believe. I believe because through belief I can say "yes" to all things, and (as ee cummings wisely said) "yes is a pleasant country." I believe because all that is seen and unseen sings out that there is someone other than myself in the universe. I believe because the yearnings in my heart and the spiritual instincts of all humanity reach out for that someone; and I believe because belief is the only courageous way of life which will help me to discover who that someone is, and how I can come to know him.

CHAPTER TWO

The Authentic Atheist

...in God the Father Almighty...

THERE IS A PICTURE of God in a painting in Ghent, Belgium. He is wearing a big crown and a red robe, he has a long beard and he is sitting on a throne. Sophisticated people and Protestants would object to this portrayal of God the Father because it is both so literal and so physical. After all, we know that God does not sit on a throne in heaven wearing a crown and a red robe. God is pure spirit. Like the jazz singer, he "ain't got no-body."

But we have to picture God somehow, and when we try to imagine a "pure spirit" all we can come up with is a bottle of vodka or rubbing alcohol. Therefore to picture God as the cosmic Father who sits on a throne as the ruler of all is probably the best image we could come up with. Some will protest that he then becomes a fairy tale king, but why is everyone so down on fairy tales? If you read the masterpiece of the splendidly named Bruno Bettleheim, *The Uses of Enchantment*, you will see that fairy tales connect humanity with the deep unconscious realm, and that's very interesting indeed. So when we imagine God as the great cosmic Father King, awefully robed and crowned, we're not being superficial but fishing deep.

We didn't think up the image of the cosmic Father King. It was given to us. It's part of humanity. It's engraved in the history of the human race. It was revealed to us as the sun mounts in the morning and as the first whisperings of love well up in a fifteen-year-old boy. That's what we call "revelation," and it is something that echoes in the human heart just about everywhere. It is that hint of something beyond and that glimpse of glory that the atheist squints not to see. Which raises some curious questions, for instance, "Why do that?"

I have a curious respect for some atheists. There is something heroic about an outspoken unbeliever. He wears his denial of God on his sleeve with a certain panache. He challenges the deity as Cyrano de Bergerac duels with death. The atheist courageously contradicts the instincts of the entire human race to declare the non-existence of God. Like a latter day Don Quixote, the atheist rides off to joust with the windmills of superstition, religion and the God of fairy tales. With touching absurdity, the crusading atheist overlooks the irony: he spends all his real time and effort refuting something he thinks is a myth. That is why I like atheists. The rebel in me always

15

admires people who paddle upstream, and should they attempt to scale a waterfall in their canoe, my admiration for them increases. The campaigning atheist is like that. Despite all the evidence, despite the universal religious instinct of the human race, he acts on his solemn belief that there is nothing to solemnly believe in. His passion wins from me a grudging respect for the militant atheist, but it also convinces me that he isn't precisely what he thinks he is. He believes too much and cares too much for truth to really be an atheist.

Is there really such a thing as an utterly authentic atheist? I think so. I have a dreadful feeling that there exists a sort of human sub-species who have lost their spiritual capacity completely. These authentic atheists do not profess belief in God, nor even disbelief. Instead they seem entirely deaf to such ideas. They do not hate the Church or say the Bible is a fairy tale. They do not spit out bigoted remarks that blame the Pope for the holocaust or missionaries for murder. They do not attack the arguments for the existence of God, say the universe is random, or call Rick Warren a simpleton. They do not rage against God, any more than someone born blind has dreams in color. These are the authentic atheists. They plod through life eating, working, shopping, breeding and sleeping, and God never seems to flit across their consciousness. Members of this sub-species may be sparkling sophisticates or ill-bred boors. They may be the decent and moral folks next door, or they could be despicable murderers. In a frightful way, it doesn't matter. If they exist, perhaps they have bred and spread like the alien bodysnatchers, and exist in our midst like spiritual zombies—indistinguishable in the teeming mass of humanity except to those few who see them and tremble.

Then there are the truly sinister atheists. These are the ones who have adopted the cruelest disguise of them all: they have become religious. They lurk in the stalls of cathedral choirs as well as the stalls of the Christmas bazaar. The religious atheists sing and speak the words of faith but do not believe in a God who is real in any sense. They worship instead a deity of their own imagining— a comfortable grandfather in the sky, or a Great Spirit who gives them pleasant dreams but makes no demands of them. The God of earthquake, wind and fire, as well as the God of the still, small voice is an alien and unreal creature to these devotees of spa religion. Whole parishes are filled with them, every Sunday.

My imagination is too vivid. I am spinning stories and jesting to make a point. Because people laugh and cry, I'm sure all humans have souls, even if they neglect them. But if my hunch is right that some people never give God a thought, then they are the best evidence that such a thing as an atheist might exist after all. If such people exist, then we are witnessing a radical and tragic decline in the human race, for it is sub-human to exist without a god of any kind. Real religion is a universal part of the human condition. In every culture and language—from primitive

tribesmen who grunt at the stars to sophisticated tech-
nicians who grunt at computer screens, the troublesome
religious instinct persists.

When you look at the human religious instinct askance,
doesn't it seem quirky and unexpected? If we are only
brutes, why this universal, tender and mysterious instinct
to fall on our faces and before our immense and intimate
Maker? If we are animals, why do we see spiritual beings
everywhere? Dogs sniff and lift their legs at trees; men
see mournful dryads imprisoned there. The real religious
instinct in man is a kind of madness, and is as unexpected,
beautiful and bizarre as those other forms of human madness called music, laughter and dance. What is this surprising inclination to worship and sing to some Almighty
Being? What instinct causes men to build an Aztec temple,
Stonehenge or Chartres, a basilica or a Baptist chapel, a
ziggurat, the Parthenon or Angkor Wat? There is virtually no human society anywhere in time or place where
religion was not somehow present. Other than the basic
social functions, is there any other phenomenon that is
more common to human beings than religion? In fact, you
could almost use the instinct and ability to pray as the
mark of what it is to be human. Perhaps we should be
called *homo orans* instead of *homo sapiens*. When a humanist
declares his independence from religion, he is not exalting
his humanity, he is lopping off an important part of it—
for the whole of human history and culture declares that a
glorious and eccentric part of being human is to seek God.

The man from Missouri reduces the wild and wonderful phenomenon of faith to the idea that God is merely the projection of humanity's need for the ultimate sugar daddy. His theory goes like this: primitive man needed to magnify ordinary authority figures like fathers and kings and project them into heaven to create an almighty being to comfort him in the face of the everlasting darkness and reward him with eternal life. In other words, the whole religious phenomenon is a huge case of corporate wishful thinking.

There are three problems with this way of thinking. First of all, it is incredibly dull. Missouri man is not the sort of person you want to go on vacation with. The second problem is that this doesn't describe the god of most religions, whose gods are not, in the main, sugar daddies who reward their children with pink clouds of cotton candy in the afterlife. Instead, they are cruel and violent supernatural beings who are more likely to devour you than delight you. Even the Christian God—who is good and paternal, and hence perhaps the closest thing to sugar and daddy—threatens final judgment and eternal damnation. This is not what I would have wished for if I were thinking wishfully. Let us stand this on its head. Given that the god of most religions is a lion, not a pussycat, perhaps it is the atheist who is engaged in wishful thinking.

There is a third problem with this line of thought, and this aspect is most disturbing. Saying God is the result of a corporate wish is a kind of bathtub-drain mentality. Everything, bubbles and scummy bath water alike, can go swirling down into it until nothing is left. The problem can be stated like this: If God is simply a case of wishful thinking, then everything good, beautiful and true might also be explained away by the same devilish logic. So, for instance, if God is the result of our wishful thinking, then morality is merely our need to impose control on our society. Patriotism becomes a projection of our bigotry and xenophobia. Beauty is no more than my own erotic urgings projected outward, and truth itself is simply my sad attempt to impose order and meaning on the chaotic and meaningless cosmos. If all is wishful thinking, then this strange phenomenon we call Love may only be a projection of our own pitiful infantile needs. If all these things are simply the projection of my own mind, then perhaps the physical world is also only real within my own perception. We know the senses can be reduced to electrical impulses to the brain. Perhaps the whole beautiful, cruel, tender and hilarious world is nothing but an electrical fizzle in my head. This is the way the world ends, not with a bang but a fizzle.

Couldn't it be that the idea of God as a projection of the human imagination is a simple reversal of the truth? The alleged atheist has strayed into a hall of mirrors and gotten lost. He's mistaken a reflection for reality. It might look like God is a projection of our imagination, but in fact we're the products of his. The ancient texts confront and correct this very problem. They warn us against making God in our own image and specifically tell us that we were made in his. Either position looks like it might be true, but then reflections do look like the real thing. Whether you think God is a projection of man or man a projection of God depends on where you start. If you start with yourself, then God is a projection, but if you start with God, then you are. This being the case, we must then ask ourselves which is the more logical starting point—you or God? Who is more likely to have been there first?

Arguing for the existence of God has always been a yawn. The most the philosophers can do is infer that God exists. But who wants to dance with an inference? Can you rage against a logical proof? Why debate the existence of light when such things as eyesight and color exist? Besides, if one has developed a believing mentality, the first step of saying not only "I believe" but also "I believe in God" may not be so difficult. However, when philosophers and New Age gurus speak of God, they use majestic and enigmatic terms like "Ultimate Being" or "Eternal Essence.. The problem with God being "Radically Other" or a "Force of Dynamism" is that we cannot imagine such a thing. It's in our nature to imagine the unimaginable using images, and when we try to picture the "Elemental Essence" or the "Spirit of Cosmic Being" we end up getting a mental image of either a huge spray of cheap perfume or a vast, astral tapioca pudding. An impersonal force seems like a sensible starting point, but most people find swimming in cosmic ectoplasm rather sticky. As a result, we soon begin to imagine the amorphous God as a personal Being. The Force receives a Face.

There is a popular theory that the idea of a personal God is primitive, while the idea of an impersonal force is sophisticated. It is imagined that simple folk believe in a personal God, but as they become wiser they come to see that God is really an impersonal force. Isn't the truth just the reverse? Isn't it more sensible to assume that it was the grunting humans emerging from the ooze who first sensed that God was a kind of ooze? Wouldn't the first religious instinct be a dim awareness that there was some sort of "impersonal force" behind all things? It was later, as man developed into a cultured, colourful, storytelling creature, that he figured out that the vague force actually had a face.

This is how infants develop. First there is the big, fuzzy, loud thing with a red spot in the middle and then as the child grows he learns to recognize his father's face, complete with beard and bulbous nose. Isn't this the way with all things and all ideas? They develop from simple to complex, and decay from complexity to simplicity. Therefore, the simpler idea that God is an impersonal force must be the more primitive. Certainly it is possible to move from faith in a personal God to acknowledgement of an impersonal force (many intellectual clergymen take this step) but such a move is always a decline, not a development. It is a slip down, not a step up.

While images for God are necessary, it is also true that all our images of God are inadequate because he is beyond both our images and our imagining. The most profound words spoken about God are the ones that remind us that we cannot speak about God. As soon as we say, "God is this," we must also say, "God is not this." But while this is true, it is also true that we can say certain things about God. We can discuss what we do not know, and we can discuss what we are discovering, and we can discuss what we hope to discover. This is what religious talk should be—a group of people who are telling stories about what they don't know about. When we tell stories, we are making complicated images of the truth in order to make sense of what is mysterious, immense and awesome. We need images to talk about God for the same reason.

Since we need images for God, the best ones are the simplest and the oldest. They are the best because they are the least likely to be taken literally. If we call God "Father," for instance, we know immediately that the image is not good enough because we think of our own hopeless, funny, and pathetic earthly fathers. The simplest and oldest images for God are also the best because they are the most universal and basic. The fact that every child in every home first knows the big, fuzzy, loud thing and then starts to laugh at his father's face, is the simplest and most beautiful reason for calling God "the Father Almighty." The Father is the first "Other" person most of us get to know. (It takes Baby a long time to figure out that "Me" and "Mommy" are actually two different people.) Therefore what could be more simple and ingenious than to call the Ultimate Other "Father"? Jesus and the Jews say this image was revealed by God Himself. The feminist anthropologists from Missouri give a more expedient explanation. They theorize that, like all other simple people, the bearded patriarchs of a patriarchal culture cast God in their own image. The Jews were bearded mini-monarchs who sat around on cushions being waited on, so they perceived God as a bearded grandfather of them all, sitting on clouds being waited on.

This is a reasonable theory, and the history of religion shows that humans have a real tendency to create gods in their own image. (Why else would the savages of the South Pacific worship the Duke of Edinburgh?) But seriously, what if this reasonable theory is also just a mirror reflection of reality? Instead of God the Father being a reflection of our fathers, what if it were the other way around? What if our own existence from our father making love to our mother rests on the fact that the whole cosmos has an ever-loving Father? What if the big bang was a masculine explosion of delight, love and creative force on a cosmic scale? What if God implanted a seed of life into all things? If so, then he really is the father of all, and that minute and precious element we call "life" is a tiny droplet of God implanted by Divine power into each and every cell of creation. If this is so, then calling God "Father Almighty" is not just an outmoded metaphor, but it is the very essence of his divine identity, an expression

24

of his connection with all things living, and an indispensable description of who he was, and is and ever shall be.

Nevertheless the intelligentsia object to God being called "Father." Could it be that, like all adolescents, they are going through a rebellious stage? Are they simply like the teenaged girl who is embarrassed when her father dances at a wedding? Do these father-phobes stomp their feet and slam their bedroom door, or do they just write a book about the evils of patriarchy? At the bottom of this entertaining dispute is the real objection to God being called "Father." To suggest that God really is, in some sense, our Father is to say that he is not only a personal God, but he is de facto in a relationship with all those whom he calls his children.

Suddenly the question of God being personal or impersonal is not an academic debating point, but an explosive question of the heart. For if God is "the Father Almighty," then I am faced with someone who cannot be ignored. An eternal force is easy enough to slight. A cosmic pudding is abstract and safe; but if the Force has a Face, then it may be looking at me, and if he is looking at me it is very possible he is looking for me. Therefore, when I say, "I believe in God the Father Almighty," I am not simply stating a truth about God, I am taking a part and stepping on stage in the midst of a melodrama of cosmic significance.

If God really is "Father," then I am in a relationship with him whether I like it or not. As Martin Buber has observed, this intimate commerce with an Other is what makes me who I am. Furthermore, I may as well cheerfully admit that, like any self-respecting adolescent, I am in a rebellious relationship with this Father. I may express the rebellion in furious rage. I may choose to ignore him in a sullen pout. Or I may choose the subtlest form of rebellion and become legalistic and pious. Finally, like the son in the famous story, I may simply choose to run away from that compelling paternal presence. In doing so, I join that dignified band of fugitives called the human race. To run away is perhaps the most honest and wholesome thing to do, and it is not wasted, for as all the great stories tell us—from the *Wizard of Oz* to the Prodigal Son—we must first run away before we can really turn toward home.

CHAPTER THREE

Of Other Worlds

...maker of heaven and earth...

Oᴺᴇ ᴏꜰ ᴛʜᴇ ɢʀᴇᴀᴛ curiosities in modern life is that so many religious people don't believe. That is to say, they disbelieve in the supernatural; and yet if religion is not supernatural, then it is not religion at all. It's something else. It's just a set of table manners. These sincere, modern people have turned religion into an ethical code or an aesthetic creed or a campaign for equal rights or a sincere attempt to make the world a better place. How dull is that?

People who deny the supernatural in religion have nothing left. Not believing in another world beyond this one, all they can do is try to make things better "down here," and in the process, what a nuisance they make of themselves! One such tiresome do-gooder was summed up in C.S. Lewis' *The Screwtape Letters*: "She's the sort of woman who lives for others—you can tell the others by their hunted expression."

No wonder so few people bother with religion these days, when the whole faith game has become merely a club for politically correct, sincere people in sandals who want to go around being nice to everyone. Believing that God is the maker of heaven and earth is far removed from such banal religiosity. This article of faith puts a petard under the polite. It shakes up all those who see only this material world and the need to improve it. A belief in heaven and earth demands a belief in other worlds and other realms, and in other beings who inhabit those realms.

So. Give me that ole' time religion with gods and angels and demons and other realities that press in on this one; give me the joy of heaven and the fear of hell. It is this full-blooded religion with a belief in other worlds and spiritual beings and a certain uncertainty that gives me a thrill in the mind and a chill of terror and delight, and makes me wonder by day and tremble by night.

In *The Universe in a Nutshell*, Professor Stephen Hawking tells us that alternative worlds are a real possibility. Fans of fantasy rejoice! Children of Narnia come out from hiding! Science fiction geeks and hobbit lovers, step from your paperback world with pride. Stepping through wardrobes, falling down rabbit holes and traveling to other worlds is possible after all! The news is out: modern physics has caught up with ancient metaphysics. Science has caught up with science fiction, and we need no longer be ashamed to believe in alternative worlds.

I realize Professor Hawking would probably not be as unreserved in his enthusiasm for Narnia, Wonderland and Middle Earth as I am. I accept that when we affirm that God is the "maker of heaven and earth," some residents of Missouri blame us for believing in fairy tales. I have played into their hands. They smile that we still believe in other worlds. We are blamed for naively believing in a three-tiered universe with heaven in the sky, earth in the middle and hell underground. But has anyone ever believed our world was really like that, or were they just telling stories? When ancient people said they believed in heaven and hell, did they really think hell was underground and heaven could be located on the other side of the clouds? I doubt it. I doubt whether ancient people who dug mines were surprised when they didn't find fiends roasting sinners in lakes of fire underground. In my experience, most religious people cope with metaphors fairly adeptly. It was the poor literal-minded cosmonaut who seemed surprised when he went to outer space and didn't see angels and God sitting on a throne.

When a person says he believes in heaven and earth, he means he accepts a material realm and a spiritual realm. The person who proposes the existence of a spiritual realm does so not because he wants to live in fantasyland, but because a spiritual realm is necessary to account for his experience. In other words, his decision to accept the spiritual realm is essentially scientific, not religious. That is to say, he has arrived at his conclusion as the result of observation and deduction. The idea of a spiritual realm provides possible explanations for all the weird and wonderful experiences which human beings keep reporting and which *Fortean Times* magazine so delightfully records.

When faced with fish falling from the sky, crop circles, visits from aliens and angels, ghosts, fairies, monsters, miracles and apparitions, the man from Missouri says such things either have "natural" explanations or that they are all in the mind. Can the borders of the mind be so easily defined? As a famous rabbi said, "Yes, the spirits are real, and the spirits are imaginary. It's just that most of us cannot imagine how real our imaginations are." Of course what seems spiritual is "in the mind." How else would the spiritual realm communicate with us? Those who believe in the heavenly or spiritual realm are simply saying that there are more realities than can be perceived with the human senses. This is common sense for any boy who has ever had a nightmare or bought a whistle that only his dog could hear.

One who believes only in the visible has no space for the invisible realm, but if I believe in all things visible and invisible, I can allow for both types of reality, and allow for strange interactions between the two. I can shrug my shoulders and make room for ghosts and ghouls as well as grace and goodness. If a spiritual realm exists, then I am not surprised at monsters or mystical experiences. Has someone seen a statue weep or bleed? Has a saintly girl's body refused to rot for a hundred years, and does it still smell like posies? Could be. Do witches cast spells that hurt people? Perhaps. Has someone been healed by the power of prayer? Have millions seen angels, watched the sun spin or seen a thousand-year-old prophecy fulfilled? Maybe. This is not to say that the believer takes all these things at face value. He is simply admitting that strange things happen. Neither does he immediately and unquestioningly accept every unusual happening as "supernatural." Like any sensible person, he knows visions are more likely if a person is insane, tired or drunk. The true believer is fully aware of how easily people are duped and deluded. When faced with an extraordinary occurrence, the ordinary believer looks for every natural explanation first. However, because the believer allows for "all things invisible," he has possible explanations for the unexplainable.

Furthermore, the person who believes in "all things visible and invisible" has got an added and interesting dimension to his life. Believing in the spiritual dimension is like putting on a pair of 3-D glasses. Everything jumps out at you. Hidden possibilities emerge. Everything surges with an inner meaning and secret life. The difference between the cynic and the believer, in this respect, is that the cynic sees *through* everything while the believer sees *into* everything. So, for example, when the cynic sees bread and wine, he sees only crushed wheat and crushed grapes, while the believer sees the crushed body of his martyred master.

The man from Missouri may warn the believer of being superstitious. He is right of course. It is possible to be superstitious, but which is better—to be superstitious or cynical? A superstitious person rarely does anyone any harm, whereas a cynical person poisons everyone he meets. There is a charming hopefulness about superstitious people. Can you actually dislike a person who kisses the bones of a saint or spends a lifetime waiting to photograph the Loch Ness monster? However, while there are some superstitious believers, there are many more who are properly skeptical of the supernatural, but not so dogmatic as to rule it out altogether. In fact, the vast majority of the human race believes in ghosts, but they do not believe their eyes when they see one. This is not superstition, but common sense. It is simply allowing, like Hamlet who saw a ghost, that there are more things in heaven and earth than Horatio's philosophy had dreamt of.

The fact of a spiritual dimension brings a personal God back into the conversation because this phrase from the creed echoes the first verse of the Hebrew creation myth, which says God is the maker of both heaven and earth. In other words, he made both the spiritual and the physical realms. The fundamentalists tell us with great solemnity that God made the heaven and the earth in one week beginning on Sunday, October 23, 4004 BC. The evolutionist tells us with an equally awed whisper that the world evolved over an unimaginably long period of time. Although the fundamentalist and the evolutionist would hate to be lumped together, their mindset is the same, because they both have to explain everything with dates and charts and time periods. The evolutionist mesmerizes us with unimaginable eons, while the fundamentalist draws realistic pictures of Adam riding a dinosaur.

The creationist and the evolutionist stand back to back like two Missouri madmen strapped together, each unaware of the other's existence. In this matter, isn't it safer to simply stand apart from them both? Shouldn't we regard them both with the curiosity, dismay and pity with which we regard all madmen? Why should we accept their self-confident statements when common sense tells us that no one can be sure how or when the world was created because no one was there when it happened? Furthermore, their grandiose theories all rely on the fixed nature of time. When people are dying, they report that their entire life is re-experienced in the most vivid way within the space of two minutes. Perhaps the whole dimension of time may be far more elastic than we thought. How do we know time is a fixed quality at all? And if time is rubbery, then everything is else is flexible too.

But our considerations of creation are not over until two fat men sing: G.K. Chesterton and Thomas Aquinas, who on this subject might belt out a duet. In *Orthodoxy*, Chesterton says this on how he discovered the Creator: "I had always believed the world involved magic: now I thought that perhaps it involved a magician. And this pointed a profound emotion always present and sub-conscious; that this world of ours has some purpose; and if there is a purpose, there is a person. I had always felt life first as a story: and if there is a story there is a storyteller."Aquinas responds, *"Quidquid fit, causam habet."* ("Whatever happens has a cause.") If you go back far enough in time, there must come a time when there is no time. There comes a Cause that had no cause. When we say in the creed that God is the maker of heaven and earth, we are simply stating the monumental fact that God is the Great Monumental Fact. He is the First Cause, the One before whom there is no other. That he made heaven and earth is what we believe. That is the poetic fact. How he did it is where prosaic fiction comes in.

It is entertaining to guess how God made the heaven and the earth, and mankind has been engaged in all kinds of storytelling to do just that down through the ages. It may well be that he spoke creation into existence one week long, long ago and said, "That's good!" after each day's work. Or perhaps he sang the heavens and earth into creation, as Aslan did Narnia. Perhaps he planned all things with the exquisite precision of an engineer, or perhaps, like some marvelous Michelangelo, he is passionately and obsessively at work on a million projects at once. Then there is the dull creation myth that says the world simply evolved into what it now is over a very long passage of time.

I'm content that God may have used some sort of evolutionary process, but what I cannot believe is that the whole of heaven and earth by chance just happened to happen. I admit to being a believer even to the point of gullibility at times, but I simply cannot make such a leap of faith. I know many people believe this miraculous story, seemingly with no problem. They accept the infallibility of their biology teachers. I have tried to believe the gospel according to Darwin, but I cannot.

With not one nudge or hint of a wink that the theory is a huge practical joke, we are supposed to believe the solemn story that the whole of creation, with its vast intricacy, evolved over billions of years simply by random chance. It looks leaky. It seems to me the theory has been pieced together with a piece of bone here and a fossil there and held together by the glue of ingenuity and the artificial awesomeness of great amounts of time. In this, I confess, I am an incurable doubter and cynic. I am in favor of leaps of faith, but I am not that athletic.

The problem with chance-driven evolution is that one is required to trust in random meaninglessness—and this from the people who blame religious folks for having "blind" faith! Do people really believe that even one simple organism can develop from a mindless sludge of mud, by chance, if one just waits long enough? If a simple organism cannot develop by chance from the primordial soup, how much less a complex organism, or the whole delicately balanced, interrelated, vastly complex and beautiful natural world? Doesn't everyday experience tell us that complex things on their own *return* to mud, not emerge from it? Doesn't common sense tell us that complexity disintegrates into simplicity, and simplicity, on its own and by random, never develops into complexity? Can anybody else spot the naked emperor here?

When I affirm that God is the maker of heaven and earth, I repudiate the idea that the whole of creation came about by chance. Happily, the creed leaves it there. As a believer I do not have to take it further than this, and as such, the believer's creed is far more flexible and open minded than the materialist's. The believer can have God and nature, but the materialist must only have nature. The believer's system, like his mind, is therefore open, while the materialist's is closed.

That God is the creator tells me not only what God did, but who he is. When I say I believe in the "maker of heaven and earth," I have discovered another image of the personal God. At the heart of his being he is a maker; a progenitor and an artist. He is a fat opera singer, a lusty painter and a tender violinist. He is an athlete, an intellectual, a poet, a gardener and a storyteller. Above all, in all and through all, he is creative and creatively alive. He is constantly making all things new, yet he has never spoken the same word of creation twice. Perhaps across the realms of time and space, throughout the universe, new worlds are springing into being. Maybe the whole fantastic work of creation is burgeoning here, there and everywhere with a prodigious, wasteful, bohemian sort of artistry. God is not a static once-and-done creator. He is a constant, creative, dynamic source, ever ancient and ever new.

Furthermore, he is a junkman, a refuse collector, a salvage expert, a recycler and a thrift store manager. Not only is he making all things fresh and new, but he is forever busy reclaiming and remaking all that was broken, lost, discarded and forlorn. He delights in turning trash into a treasure. He collects the cast-offs, recycles the wrecks and redeems the ruined, clapped-out remnants of creation. He is economical and wasteful at the same time—spending an enormous amount to recover one pearl, one treasure lost in a field, one wedding ring or one child lost in the crowded and wicked world.

If he is the maker of heaven and earth, then he is also the maker of me, for I am a part of heaven and earth. Indeed I am one of those hybrid marvels called humans, in which heaven and earth are jumbled together in a heady and maddening mixture. He has made me from dust but breathed into me the breath of Life. I believe in the Maker of heaven and earth because I see heaven and earth in conflict not only all around me, but also within me. I can feel the clash of brute beast and everlasting beauty. This war between heaven and earth is constant and severe. The strife in me has broken my heart. I'm one of the walking wounded. I leak. But if he is not only the artist, but also the salvage expert, it means there is hope, because he might rescue and restore me. Therefore, to paraphrase Oscar Wilde, although I lie in the gutter, I may look up to contemplate the stars. (*Lady Windermere's Fan.*) Although I am a creature of earth, I am also a child of heaven, and the hound of that heaven may one day find me and lead me on the long journey home.

CHAPTER FOUR

The Scandal of Particularity

...and in Jesus Christ, his only Son,
our Lord...

VICTORIAN DESIGNERS OF stained glass windows have a lot to answer for. Enshrined forever in their sumptuous art is the picture of gentle Jesus meek and mild. He has blond hair, a sweet smile, and a glowing halo and he is wearing rich robes that the Jewish carpenter from a hick town in Palestine must have somehow borrowed from one of the Emperor's courtesans.

This blond-haired, blow-dried Germanic Jesus presented in the stained glass windows of our great grandfathers is not only a travesty of who Jesus Christ really is, but this image (supported by endless Bible story books with similarly simpering illustrations) has effectively inoculated generations of Christian children against any real encounter with Jesus Christ. Rather than meeting a real person (by, for example, reading one of the four gospels), generations of Christians have imagined that their Lord is some sort of supernatural pansy who never quite gets his sandals dirty. Consequently, he can be written off as an illustration in a story book, a beautiful work of art and therefore the figment of the imagination of those weird and impractical people called "artists."

The Christian faith springs not from this beautifully robed and coiffed effeminate man,but from the birth, life and death of a real Jewish teacher from a backwater town in the backwoods of a backward province in the Roman Empire. Jesus Christ was the equivalent of a country revivalist preacher with a podunk accent and a sharp line in hellfire, brimstone and healing. No wonder the snooty religious folks in their fine robes didn't like him. In fact, they didn't like him so much that they eventually turned him into one of themselves, combed his hair, put him in fancy robes and immortalized him in neo-gothic stained glass windows. That did away with him far more effectively than something so crude as a crucifixion.

Jesus Christ was a real human being who, the Christian faith also insists, was God in human form. There's a radical, eye popping, jaw-dropping belief for you, and one which will take some chewing over if you're to make progress....

One Autumn afternoon I went for a walk with a Buddhist monk. This young man from Australia had all the cool reserve and lofty detachment one expects of a man in his trade. We discussed monasticism and meditation and found much in common. Then we began to discuss what we actually believed. The Buddhist had been cool. Suddenly he went cold. While he'd been happy to discuss his karma, he wasn't happy to explain his dogma. When the conversation turned to the topic of God, I tiptoed up to the idea of a personal God. The Buddhist understood the proposition, but didn't think it a probability. When I told him that Christians actually believe the transcendent God took particular human form, in a unique way at a particular place and time the Buddhist drifted into a polite silence. I was embarrassed. I felt as if I had exposed my gullibility, committed an error in taste, or maybe even a blasphemy.

The intelligent Buddhist is sensible to shy away from the idea that the personal God took human form in Jesus Christ. Buddhists aren't the only ones. Indeed there are plenty of Christians who also shy away from this most robust and embarrassing of doctrines. I respect their honesty. In fact, the Christians I suspect are the smiling, squeaky-clean ones who seem to have no problems with the incredible idea that God became a particular person in Palestine two thousand years ago. I worry because if they don't have a problem, I wonder if they have ever really thought it through. If they haven't, they are at best beginners and perhaps even bogus believers, because when it comes to the idea of the Incarnation, most honest believers have honest doubts.

The intellectually outrageous idea that God jumped on the roller coaster of the human race is called "the scandal of particularity." With this term the theologians raise their hand and admit that it is an intellectual embarrassment to suppose that a transcendent God would step into human history and be born of a peasant girl in a smelly stable in a backwater of the Roman Empire around 7 BC. I take their point. Like the sheep in the stable, I feel sheepish when I view the Christ child. I find myself a bit envious of the Buddhist whose religion isn't encumbered with something as embarrassing as an incarnation.

But what is embarrassing is often true. That's why it's embarrassing. What embarrasses us also kicks us awake. When the parish priest turns out to have a fondness for Elvis Presley impersonation, we are surprised, delighted, dismayed and curious to know more. Furthermore, if we know anything about the priest, it suddenly fits. The truth clicks into place. So that's why he takes so many holidays to Nashville and dyes his hair black! That's why the housekeeper spotted a corset in his closet and a pair of sequined bell-bottoms in the bottom drawer!

There is something wild and unpredictable about truth. When everything is cut and dried (like hair and flowers), don't you suspect that you're being offered something attractive, but artificial? Buddhism, for example, is a most attractive religion. It is exactly the sort of religion one would make up if one had to. It makes sense. It is cautious. It is controlled, rational and pure. Real Christianity, on the other hand, is none of that. It is particular and unpredictable, contradictory and messy. It stands the staid religions on their heads. This is the maddening and delightful thing about Christianity; because it's upsetting and awkward, it's real. That's why Christianity feels more true than Buddhism, because it is more like life itself—quirky, colorful, comic, tragic and true.

If truth is always stranger than we expect, it is also more ordinary than we expect, (and that's what is most strange about it). Once we've seen that something is true (no matter how strange it seemed at first), it becomes as common and real as baked beans or bicycles. It belongs. It fits. Furthermore, if it is a central truth, then it not only fits, but everything fits around it. A central truth not only makes sense, but it makes sense of everything else. So, for instance, if you didn't know better, your everyday experience of life would lead you to conclude that the world was flat. But then one day someone tells you that the world is round. You might find this difficult to believe, since it contradicts what your experience has told you all along, but when you take the leap of faith and accept that the world is round and not flat, then everything else suddenly makes more sense too. "So that's why the sailors wind up where they started!"

A similar thing happens when we contemplate the idea that the eternal God could become one particular person in human history. Our whole instinct leads us to deny such a preposterous proposition. But why should the idea

that a universal becomes particular necessarily be so difficult? How could the universal be real if it did not become
particular? As the old washerwoman replied when she was
asked what she was thinking, "How do I know what I'm
thinking unless I says it?" It is the nature of everything
unspoken, vague, invisible and universal to be particularized. In fact, when you see it this way, isn't it more of a
scandal if the universal does not become particular?

All around us we see the miracle of the universal becoming particular over and over again. So, for example,
the universal principles of music become particular when
Charlotte sits down to play Chopin. At that point we do
not think it scandalous that the great universal music has
become limited to a particular combination of keys on a
particular keyboard played by a particular set of ten fingers and heard by a particular pair of ears. Indeed, if the
music were not particularized in this way, we would never
know music at all. Furthermore, to be real, the music has
to be made particular over and over again. The miracle of
the universal music becoming a Chopin etude, a jazz riff
or a Broadway tune is always and every place the miracle
of the universal becoming uniquely particular.

But we are talking about God, not Gershwin, and the
main reason we perceive a problem with God becoming
particular is because he is supposed to be "up there" while
we are "down here." But this way of looking at heaven
and earth isn't big enough. It isn't small enough either.
Blake saw the world in a grain of sand and heaven in a

wildflower. He held heaven in the palm of his hand and eternity in an hour. For him, the universal was particular all over the place, and that was the definition of it being universal. The visible and the invisible are not separated into "up there" and "down here." The universal and the particular are intermingled all the time and in every place, from the vast reaches of outer space to the microscopic reaches of every cell.

Doesn't all the evidence point to this conclusion? All of creation has its predictable visible element tumbled together with a surprising invisible element. In physics, Bell's Theorem assures us that there are connections inside reality that cannot be explained by the normal categories of touch, contact and contiguity. Things affect each other in ways that go beyond the usual categories of physical causality. As soon as the scientists explain one part of the physical realm, some vast or minute mystery opens up, and an unexpected inconsistency makes them think again.

If the visible and invisible are commingled in this mysterious way, why should we suppose that God is totally separate from the physical world he created? This is not to say that the created world is God, nor that it contains God, or that God depends on the world he created. It is just that he is not absent from it. While he exceeds it, he is also inside it. He is both the force that made it and the force that holds it together. If God exists with, and in, and through the physical realm, then why is it so difficult to believe that he might emerge from that realm and take a particular physical form at a particular place and time? It is only a more specific focus of the kind of presence he has always maintained in the world. We imagine the incarnation as Jesus coming down from heaven to this world like an alien or an angel. It seems more probable to me that he was here all along, and that he simply decided to step out from the crowd.

This putting on of human flesh seems astounding to us because we imagine that God is totally spiritual, and by "spiritual" we mean ethereal and well—clean! He must regard the physical world as distasteful and dirty. We imagine that becoming incarnate is for God a strange and disagreeable activity—that to do so he might have to wrinkle his nose and put on rubber gloves. But what if the truth is exactly the other way around? Maybe God enjoys becoming incarnate. Maybe part of God's personal nature is a curious delight in dressing up. Maybe he puts on human flesh with the same seriousness and whimsy as an actor puts on his broad hat, hose and rubber nose to play Cyrano de Bergerac and save the wounded world. Maybe that was part of the poem when Joseph put on his luxurious colored coat. Maybe in countless worlds throughout the universe, God is putting on the garment of flesh in a multitude of forms we can never imagine. Maybe he prepares each world for his incarnation in gradual, creative ways and means, as he did through the rough and tumble family history of the Hebrews in our world.

Religious historians make the point that the myth of the incarnate God was commonplace amongst the ancient peoples. Practically every religion had stories of incarnate gods and goddesses. Some actually had myths about gods who took human form, then died and rose again to save the world. The early Christians simply adopted the current religious language and mythology, say the comparative religionists. But similarity does not demand connection or causality. I am not descended from or related to all other bald-headed men with large noses. The similarities within religions do not disprove the Christian story. If anything, just the reverse. The fact that the Christian story echoes the earlier stories suggests that the older, more tentative stories were simply a rehearsal for the real thing. The similarity between the Christian story and other incarnation tales is not surprising or incredible. What would be surprising and incredible would be for the Christian story not to have any shared characteristics with other world religions. The fact that it does validates its authenticity and universality.

Still we are told that the myth of the incarnation cannot be a historical fact. It is simply a religious myth like all the others. The problem with that theory is that the story of Jesus Christ doesn't actually read like a myth. Unlike the great religious myths, the gospel story is rooted in ordinary people and real places. Even if it can be shown that the gospel writers differed on the details, the whole point was that they bothered with the details at all.

Some people say the devil is in the details, but for the gospel writers, that's where the divine was. Their intent, and the point of the whole New Testament, was to show that God had taken flesh as a particular historical person, a Jewish rabbi from Nazareth called Jesus. If only the gospel writers hadn't told us about particular Roman rulers and particular towns in Judea, we could sigh with relief and write the whole thing off as yet another lovely myth.

The scandal of this particularity is shocking because of its humility. How could God who is above all, and is not dependent on any created thing, come into the world and be dependent on a Jewish peasant girl for his every need? "Did God cry for a breast of milk, then burp, smile and gurgle?" asks the man from Missouri. The Christian shrugs his shoulders, gives an embarrassed grin and says, "That's where the logic leads." The curious thing is that we struggle with such a concept. We think such condescension contradicts God's essential nature, but what if it were the other way around, and this act of humility does not contradict, but confirms God's essential nature? What if this act, above all others, reveals exactly what God is like? What if those countless Madonnas holding a Christ child for us to view are the clearest picture we will ever get of God himself? Wouldn't that be a crazy and wonderful surprise, after all those tiresome thunder gods and devouring earth mothers—all those Obi Wan Kenobi Forces-That-Are-With-You or the distant deities of the East?

To turn things on their head, it is that hiccupping infant who shows us what real power is like. While he is independent of his creation, this God chose to burst that truth from the inside out, limit himself by place and time and put Himself at the mercy of his creatures. We said he was the Ultimate Father. Here he is the Ultimate Child. The man from Missouri dislikes paradox, but a paradox always slaps us awake with a new perception of truth. Saying we "believe in Jesus Christ, his only Son, our Lord" means that while God remains the Master, he takes the form of a slave. The Almighty becomes All Meek. Furthermore, it is by giving up his sovereign power that he actually confirms it most strikingly. Anyone can cling to power. Only the omnipotent can pick it up and put it down at will—and yet his will still is done.

This is the mark of the truly great—that it can become small. We call this virtue humility, and we are surprised that God is humble. To be humble is not to be a groveling peasant or a sniveling simpleton. Humility is the radiant quality of being totally and utterly oneself—in other words, it is not being a simpleton, but being simple. God must by nature be simple. In other words, he must be completely one and completely himself without any duplicity or complication. If he is himself, then he is humble, and the logical action of his humility is for him to take the lowest possible form while still retaining his essential image. If this is the case, then for God to take particular human form is not an arbitrary act of charity on the part of an essentially aristocratic deity; it is the essential act of a humble deity. In other words, for God to become a human being actually fulfills one dimension of who God is. In that sense, what we call the miracle of the Incarnation is as natural as water flowing downhill.

This scandalous doctrine therefore confirms God's power rather than contradicting it. The fact that we call Jesus Christ "God's Son" is the historical reality that confirms and consolidates God's reputation. It is his calling card, his résumé, his *pièce de résistance*. This reversal of our preconceptions stands the whole world upside down. If God became man in a village of Palestine two thousand years ago, then the whole way I look at myself and my world is changed. Suddenly, the heart of religion is not about formulas and forms, rituals, rules and regulations. It is about becoming real—as real and particular as God did. Suddenly, religion is not about dull conformity, but radical nonconformity. It is not about fitting in, but sticking out, for if everyone else is seeking to be a little god, then to be a little person is to be a non-conformist. Perhaps this is what the man-child meant when he said we had to become like little children to enter his kingdom. So if I want to be like God (which after all, is only human nature) then I will look for the path of simplicity. I will find ways to be totally and honestly myself. Furthermore, I will seek out those who are also simple and simply themselves. I will also find ways to serve without counting the cost, and seek sacrifice without reward. This is why the saints show us what God is like while sinners only show us what they are like. The saint is someone who has discovered the secret of becoming like God. She has learned to lower herself in imitation of the incarnation. Saying, "I believe In Jesus Christ, his only Son, our Lord" is not the dull recitation of an outmoded dogma. It is a dramatic means of plunging headfirst into this scandalous and beautiful belief. It means getting my hands dirty and becoming more particular and more real than I ever imagined. It means becoming all that I was meant to be. Do you want to be real? Then contemplate the Incarnation, for the mystery of the Incarnation proclaims the beautiful truth that reality is below you and within you, not above and beyond you. Do you want to find God? Then contemplate the Incarnation. It is the living proof of that universal principle that you must go down to meet God, for God always comes to us from below, and we must stoop and kneel to find him.

CHAPTER FIVE

Arians, Apollinarians and One Eyed Pirates

...who was conceived by the Holy Spirit...

T HE DIFFERENCE BETWEEN a doubt and a difficulty is that a person with a doubt says, "That can't be!" and the person with a difficulty says, "How can that be?" In other words, the person with a doubt is a doubter. He's a cynic. He's the man from Missouri. He does not believe because he cannot, and he cannot because he will not. The person with a difficulty, however, is one who wants to believe and does, but simply can't figure it out yet.

John Henry Newman said, "A thousand difficulties do not make a doubt." In other words, we're talking about a condition of the will, not a crisis of the intellect. The person with a difficulty, like a child, believes and trusts implicitly. Then he asks the questions in order to get the answers, and he accepts them even if they are too strange to fully understand. The person indulging doubt, on the other hand, asks questions in order to shoot down the answers.

So it was in that the early Christians accepted the idea that Jesus Christ was the God-Man; then they tried to figure out just what that meant and just how it could be and just what the implications were and just how they were going to explain it to the ordinary folk in the pews. They argued and fought and finally figured it out, and as they did, they not only pre-empted an awful lot of later religious debate, but also opened up a new understanding not only of Jesus Christ, but a new understanding of humanity and God and everything.

Every argument is a theological argument, and so it all (in the end) comes down to some intriguing debates on the level of philosophy and theology—intriguing debates that, at the heart of all things, have an impact on me and you and our ultimate destiny.

When the pope visited Athens and was met with religious riots in the streets, he was taking part in a venerable Greek religious tradition. The Greeks have been rioting over religion for centuries. It is a wonderful and eccentric part of their culture. It may seem odd to us that the Greeks riot over arcane matters like the primacy of the Bishop or Rome or the double procession of the Holy Spirit; but the Greeks probably think it odd that the English take to the streets in the passionate defense of a fox, or that Americans take to the streets with marching bands and majorettes to honor their homecoming queen.

Compared to the icy disdain most Anglo-Saxons nurture toward any form of religious enthusiasm, the Greeks' passion for a theological riot seems as gutsy and wholesome as their taste for goat's cheese and olives washed down with ouzo, or their habit of breaking crockery at weddings. Down through the ages, the Greeks have rioted over religious truth because they believed religious truth was not only possible, but important. In the third and fourth centuries, the early Christians, like all brothers and sisters, fought bitterly. Like siblings quarreling over a will, they fought over their theological inheritance, and the conclusions mattered because the result of the battle determined what kind of world their children would inherit.

The debates centered on just what exactly the birth, life and death of Jesus Christ really meant. But this was not simply a matter of theological nit-picking. The Greeks—natural philosophers that they are—understood that the answers affected everything. The debates were conducted by colorful characters: prelates, politicians, emperors and archbishops. The quarrels were complicated by philosophy and theology, politics and power, but beneath the fascinating details there were really only two sides to the debate, and these two sides recur in virtually every philosophical debate. Put simply, they are illustrated in the famous Raphael painting "The School of Athens." In the center stand the philosophers Aristotle and Plato. Aristotle points down to the earth and Plato points up to the heavens. Aristotle thought earthly realities more real than heavenly realities, while Plato thought the heavenly realities more real than the earthly.

When the early Christians asked who Jesus really was, they were given the answer by Jesus' immediate followers that he was God in human flesh. But when they got the simple answer that Jesus was God incarnate, they wanted to define just how Jesus was God in human flesh, and that's when the fight broke out. The quarrel was the usual clash between heaven and earth. Was Jesus a man who seemed godlike, or a god who seemed manlike? Was he a very good man, but not fully God, as a teacher called Arius claimed, or was Apollinarius right that Jesus was fully God but not fully human? On one side the Arians, like Aristotle, pointed to the earth. On the other side the Apollinarians, like Plato, pointed to heaven. Don't imagine that this is arcane, antique, esoteric and irrelevant. The clash between heaven and earth, between the universal and the particular, the visible and invisible, matter and spirit affects the way we view ourselves, other people and everything. In other words, what we think about matter *matters*.

The clash between the two points of view seemed irreconcilable, but in any irreconcilable quarrel, the way through is for both sides to admit they are wrong, and then for both sides to admit that they are right. In other words, both sides are partially right and partially wrong. To find the truth, we have to genuinely see both sides and embrace both truths, even if doing so seems contradictory or paradoxical. The truth, therefore, is always stereoscopic. Error, on the other hand, has single vision. That is why pirates always wear eye patches.

I have spent some time discussing ancient philosophers, combative Greeks and one-eyed pirates because it all has to do with the little phrase "conceived by the Holy Spirit." In the debates about who exactly Jesus Christ was, the ones who were piratical were heretical. In other words, the heretics were one-eyed. They could only see one truth and not the other. So the Arians affirmed that Jesus was truly man, but denied that he was truly God. The Apollinarians affirmed that he was truly God, but denied that he was truly man.

This ancient debate matters because these two opposing points of view stand as symbols for almost every category of debate. So in our distorted age, the greedy materialist believes only in the physical realm, while the gullible spiritualist believes only in the spiritual realm. All these errors, whether ancient or modern, spiritualist or scientific, point up the difficulty in reconciling the spiritual realm and the material. This clash between the invisible and the visible is the very stuff of religion, and any faith that avoids the conflict misses the point. Neither is the conflict confined to the realm of philosophy and theology. Religion is both about God in heaven and the idiot next door. Religion involves my prayer book and my bankbook, my sex life as well as my prayer life. The conflict is there, because in me and in everyone else, there is a creature of earth and air struggling for flesh and spirit to be reconciled.

The Greeks rioted in the streets because they realized how important it is to resolve the clash between heaven and earth. I was taught that the whole world hung on the principles of physics. Now I believe the whole world hangs on the principles of metaphysics. If the spiritualists are right, then this world doesn't matter, but if the materialists are right, nothing but this world matters. Ironically, the results of both views are the same, for if this world doesn't matter, I can do what I like, but likewise, if there is nothing but this world, I may also do what I like, for there is no hell to pay. In other words, if I am seeing like a pirate, I may end up behaving like a pirate.

This clash between heaven and earth is solved by the conception of a child who was both fully God and fully human. In Jesus Christ a physical birth solved a metaphysical problem. In biology, conception means the fusion of two individuals into one, and in the biological theology of Christianity it means the fusion of two worlds into one. At the core of this concept is the belief that at a particular place and time, heaven and earth were merged. The universal and immortal became particular and mortal; outer space entered inner space, the timeless entered time, and that which is spiritual and divine penetrated that which was physical and human. This point of fusion banishes all confusion. The old categories of spiritual and temporal, physical and spiritual, heavenly and earthly are abolished. Christians believe that God hovered over a young woman and conceived a new being—a fusion of heaven and earth—the one called both Son of Man and Son of God. As the ancients observed, in Jesus Christ we do not have merely a good man, but the god-man.

One of the things he said was that a seed had to fall into the ground and die in order to bring new life. He was that seed. In that new man, a little droplet of heaven was planted in earth. As a result, a new relationship between earth and heaven exists. The old dualities are irrelevant. A new world order is possible. Because of the ultimate implications of this astounding insight, it was vitally important to get the details of this dogma right. That is why the stubborn Bishop Athanasius in the fourth century insisted on the problematic and paradoxical formula that Jesus Christ was fully God and fully man. A compromise would have been far simpler. A "new form of words" could have made peace, but any other form of words would not have expressed what the first Christians truly believed had happened. Then they remembered that he had said himself that he came not to bring peace, but a sword. The fusion of God and man in Jesus Christ reconciled earth and heaven, but it also divided humanity into those who accepted the reconciliation and those who refused to be reconciled. The early Christians understood that only a fully stereoscopic vision of Jesus as the God-Man would reconcile the opposing factions and change the world forever. If Jesus Christ was only a good man, then the world had not changed. If he was God who only seemed to be a man, then again, the world had not changed. But if Jesus Christ is truly God and truly man, then a bit of heaven had been planted in earth and the clash between heaven and earth was over forever. Suddenly Plato and Aristotle could embrace one another. The chasm was bridged, the wound was healed, the war was over.

This is why Christianity in its full-blooded rumbustious dogma is subversive and revolutionary—not because it preached freedom for slaves or because the martyrs refused to swear allegiance to the Emperor; not because beautiful virgins and venerable old men went to heroic deaths or because Jesus taught people to be meek and mild. All these things had happened before and elsewhere. Christianity was revolutionary because it taught that in Jesus Christ there was a stunning new relationship between all things visible and invisible.

This is why Christianity is unique among world religions. Every other religion tries to bridge the gap between earth and heaven through some technique. Some call for their devotees to make bloody sacrifices to please the gods and get them to come down. Others call for the flesh to be subdued by obedience to a strict law code. Others call for their followers to forget the suffering of the flesh in order to achieve a higher consciousness. In each case, they try to bridge the gap between flesh and spirit, but in Christianity the gap is bridged for us. It is accomplished at the moment that the Holy Spirit conceives the god-man.

This reconciliation also explains the curious contradictory nature of Christianity. Christians have always insisted that both the flesh and the Spirit are good. Christian monks may punish the flesh through fasting, but they also pamper the flesh with feasting. The Church teaches the virtue of celibacy, then turns around and praises marriage, making love and making babies. She makes religious laws, then says it is love, not laws that matter. Christians are happy to kiss both the tattered robe of St. Francis and the embroidered cope of the bishop. They kneel in both the hovel where Christ was born and the cathedral where he is adored. Christians are taught to love their bodies and laugh at them. In other words, they are trained to keep their eyes firmly on heaven and their feet firmly on earth. Through the reconciliation of heaven and earth, the Christian constantly realizes that the spiritual and the physical are intertwined. It is as if the heavenly lady and the earthly gentleman were forever spinning like Fred Astaire and Ginger Rogers.

Because of this interplay between the physical and the spiritual, it sounds that the Christian way is like walking a tightrope between the excesses of the flesh and the excesses of the Spirit. This is not the case. The Christian way is more like the trapeze than the tightrope. We are not called to tread a delicate balance between the spiritual and the physical, but to leap off the platform and fly through the air, borne up by the strong arms of both.

The conception that fused earth and heaven was accomplished by the power of God that Christians call the Holy Spirit. The Holy Spirit is not some weak ghostly figure that floats about like ectoplasm. Instead it is that fiery, chthonic force that rumbles at the heart of creation from the dawn of time. The first words of the Book of Genesis hint that the same brooding, gestating and conceiving power was there at the beginning. The Holy Spirit constantly broods over the bent world to bring forth new life. Those who wanted a Force have got one. The Holy Spirit is, as Dylan Thomas put it, "the force that through the green fuse drives the flower." He is, according to Gerard Manley Hopkins, "the dearest freshness deep down things". He is there, pressing like an impatient lover to infuse every life and enthuse the whole world. That same creative force is not just there—it has direction. It has purpose. It has a goal to reach. "The force that drives the water through the rocks drives my red blood." (Thomas again) It broods over the chaotic darkness of my life not forever and for no reason, but right now and for a purpose. As it conceived a fusion of earth and heaven in the god-man, so the same Spirit writhes and wrestles to reconcile earth and heaven in me. It blazes forth to guide me from my alpha to my unimaginable omega. That power which conceived the god-man conceives all things and brings them forth through pain to new and everlasting life. My task and my calling is listen to that voice and follow that calling, so that my life of earth and clay may one day be reconciled among the stars.

CHAPTER SIX

Purity is Power

...and born of the Virgin Mary...

I S THERE ANYTHING in our human nature and our human society that we are more confused about than sex? After all, the sexual act is simply a natural function by which we procreate, and yet this simple and exquisite action is loaded with profound levels of pleasure and perversion. It's loaded with stupidity and silliness as well as philosophical meaning and psychological depths. The urge for pleasure becomes twisted and obsessive. We become sex-haunted, and the desire, being twisted, soon twists everything else. It makes us delirious with desire and langorous with longing. It causes us to behave with a kind of Dionysian madness and risk everything for one fleeting, illicit pleasure.

Therefore, it comes as a surprise that this most elemental, below the belt, visceral, hot, juicy and dangerous aspect of the human experience is locked in at the heart of the Christian creed, for this little phrase that mentions the Virgin Mary touches not only on the one we call the Mother of God, but on the whole vast topic of human life and love. It does so because, as we contemplate the Virgin Mary, we behold the one who is the answer to the maelstrom of emotions and urges that we call sexuality. She is the beauty to our beast. She is the eye of the storm. She is the little child who charms the monster. She is Aurora—the first light of dawn in the midst of the dark. She is a draft of spring water in the desert heat. Her bright normalcy reveals our depravity, and her simple modesty and plain humility reveal our proud and complex bestiality.

This is why, down through the ages, the Blessed Virgin Mary has held the fascination of the human race. She unlocks something supernaturally natural within the human heart. She shows us what we might become. Through a mysterious transaction, she not only shows every man his true potential; she also provides the power from her purity to help that Everyman ascend to become the Everlasting Man.

Last year I visited the National Gallery of Art in Washington D.C. The gallery consists of a classical-style building where they display paintings, and a vast geometric sprawl of a building that houses modern art. I decided to start off exploring the modern collection. Red leatherette drainpipes were stuck on the wall, a plastic box held fruit pies made out of plaster, enormous mobiles hung from the ceiling, and the floor was littered with carved shapes like some gigantic baby had left his blocks lying around. The walls displayed huge canvases—all wonderfully colorful, anarchic and meaningless.

In fact, it was rather tame. I was surprised not to find three tons of carved animal fat, a pile of trash or a squashed hat. Where was the dog turd collection? Where was the slattern's unmade bed? Why couldn't I see a desiccated sheep in a tank of formaldehyde, a two-headed monkey or Jack the Ripper's undershirt? An authentic modern art gallery is supposed to be a cross between a porn shop, a freak show and an insane asylum, isn't it? In that sense, the modern wing of the Washington gallery was a letdown.

I decided to talk to the gallery guard instead. He was a young black guy with a suspicious eye and a smart grin. I asked him what gallery he liked best. He said he preferred the early Italian stuff. So I asked if he had a favorite painting. He smiled and suggested I find the Small Cowper Madonna. I took his suggestion and made my way to a room half full of paintings by Raphael. There in one corner hung an exquisite painting of the Madonna and Child. Raphael is famous for his Madonnas, but this one was smaller than most. It was more intimate, and the beauty more immanent. The setting conveyed all the natural innocence and simplicity of a woman with her child; but somehow this one was different. Mary's enigmatic expression and the luminosity of the colors hinted at the extraordinary mystery that was locked within that most ordinary scene. I was captivated. For a moment, time was transposed into eternity, and the mysterious theory that God at one point took human flesh was concrete and real in that mixture of pigment and paint on a piece of canvas.

It made me wonder later why we consider anything to be beautiful at all. Why should we look at a landscape, a painting or another human being and feel that surge of delight, wonder and desire which we call "beauty"? Modern aesthetic theory follows the old wives and says, "Beauty is in the eye of the beholder." But what if it is the other way around, and beauty is actually in the thing we are beholding? Isn't that what our experience tells us? We see a sunset, a Raphael Madonna or a beauty queen and we don't say, "As I regard that object, my cultural and educational background has conditioned me to interpret my inner feelings as something called beauty." Instead, we gasp and say, "That's beautiful!" Beauty is not in the eye of the beholder, but in the essence of the beheld. That's why we all feel that beauty takes us outside ourselves and puts us into contact with something greater, more mysterious and wonderful than we thought existed before.

In a way, that picture of the incarnation of God also says something about every painting and poem and piece of music that aspires to be beautiful. The object of art particularizes beauty. It makes beauty real and physical. That Raphael painting is full of grace and truth, and I beheld its glory. That's what Christians say about the relationship between Jesus and God. He incarnates beauty, truth, grace and glory. In him all beauty, truth, grace and glory come alive.

As I gazed on that luminous Madonna I made contact not only with something beautiful, but with Beauty. It was also an astoundingly intimate experience of purity and power. For a moment, I caught a glimpse of a kind of purity which was both as soft as moonlight and as hard as diamonds. I suddenly realized that purity, like all things beautiful and refined, is an acquired taste. Like the fragile beauty of a Mozart aria, or the calm, exquisite beauty of a Chinese vase, purity can only be fully sensed by those who pursue purity themselves, and this realization made my own sordid and tepid life seem small. While looking at the naked child and the Madonna's subtle smile I also realized that purity is a hidden and subtle virtue—available only to those who have been given the eyes to see.

But as soon as I speak the word "purity," I am aware of a certain sang-froid. Don't you curl up a little at the word "purity"? I do. Like most people, I am embarrassed and confused by the concept. I find that the mere word conjures up images of the "pure" girls of my youth, who were all long skirts, buckteeth and big Bibles. The Raphael Madonna stunned me with real purity, and I realized we are confused about the subject because we have been blinded by false images. We confuse purity with naiveté. We are amused and embarrassed by a kind of "aw shucks" purity which consists of grinning boys with Brylcreamed hair, girls in bobby sox, bubble gum and "Let's go out to the ballgame." We are rightly embarrassed by a false vision of purity that is the product of black-and-white TV programs where the married couples sleep in twin beds. This is not purity in all its magnificent power. It is Pollyanna purity.

If we confuse purity with wholesome naiveté, we also confuse it with grim puritanism. The word "purity" summons up the images of hatchet-faced nuns stalking the corridors of concentration-camp convent schools. When we hear "purity," we think of a squeaky-clean fundamentalist college with a sincere but sinister agenda. The word "purity" gives us nightmares of the black-and-white world of the Puritans, with their big black hats, big black books and big black witch-hunts. This kind of "purity" points an accusing claw at all those sordid "sins against purity" which haunt the adolescent conscience. So "purity," instead of being an image of shallow goodness, has been hijacked and twisted to become a tool of repression, guilt, and sour religion.

We also confuse purity with celestial otherworldliness. We think of Botticelli angels and cultivate a vague notion of a lofty, unstained realm of existence where the saints and angels sit together in unimaginable (and possibly boring) bliss on a lavender cloud. If we're really unlucky, our false religion mixes all three false images so that the cruelty of puritanism has a gloss of the grinning pollyanna along with the sentimentality of pastel angels. It doesn't take long to realize that the concept of purity has been so twisted in our modern minds that it almost doesn't exist. And yet, when we say in the creed that Jesus Christ was "born of the Virgin Mary," we are saying that he came into the world through a stupendous kind of purity that makes all our shallow concepts seem puerile. When we say in the creed that Christ was "born of the Virgin Mary," we embrace the fact that in a Jewish girl in Nazareth two thousand years ago, there existed a new matrix of purity and power, the like of which had not been seen in the world since the dawn of time.

Mary the mother of Jesus is an icon of beauty and purity because she is a virgin. But I am aware that this term, too, has been misunderstood and maligned. We think of a virgin simply as a person who has not had sexual intercourse. This is the shallowest of definitions. Defining a "virgin" as someone who has not had sexual intercourse is like defining a person from Iowa as someone who has never been to Paris. It may be true that most Iowans have not been to Paris, but to define an untraveled Iowan by that simple negative definition is too small. Even the most stay-at-home hayseed is bigger than a negative definition.

When the early Christians venerated the Virgin Mary they were honoring far more than the biological fact that a girl was intact. For them, the Virgin was not just an untouched maid. Her physical virginity was a sign of something far more. It was an indication of her whole character. In her they sensed a virginity that was a positive, potent virtue, not a negative naiveté. Mary represented all that was real, whole, and simple. She stood for everything, to paraphrase ee cummings, that was natural, that was infinite, that was "yes." Mary was a virgin in the same way that we call a forest "virgin." A virgin forest is fresh and natural, majestic and mysterious. Mary's virginity was not simply the natural beauty and innocence of a teenage girl. It held the primeval purity of Eden and the awesome innocence of Eve.

This is precisely why the earliest theologians called the girl from Nazareth the second Eve. The myth of the innocent first Mother projects an image of Woman in all her primal power and radiant beauty. Eve was at once imperious and innocent, stupendous and simple. She was the Queen of Eden and the girl next door. If we were to meet Eve, we would meet a woman who held in herself the monumental innocence of nature—as majestic as a mountain and as tender as a rose; as splendid and fragrant as the snows of the Himalayas and as joyful and free as a month-old lamb.

When the theologians of the second century called the Virgin Mary the second Eve, they were implying that by a special act of God she had been created without the usual human tendency to choose evil. This freedom of choice gave humanity a second chance. In the primal myth the first innocent woman said "no" to God and "yes" to herself. The girl of Nazareth was a new chance for humanity to say "no" to itself and "yes" to God. Mary's innocence and purity were of the same order as Eve's. In her, virginity is not just a physical fact, but a metaphysical truth. In her, creation was fresh and new again, and because of this seed of innocence, the opportunity was given for every morsel of creation to one day be born again.

You might imagine that such total innocence and goodness would make Mary a sort of Galilean wonder woman. It's true that her innocence was extraordinary, but it was also very simple. That is to say that while it was momentous, it did not seem remarkable at the time. There is a curious twist to real innocence. It is summed up by the observation that what is natural is not unusual. If a person is innocent, then they are as they should be. There is nothing bizarre or eccentric about them. There is therefore nothing that calls attention to them. Innocent people are at home with themselves, and no one is out of place when they are at home. In the countryside Mother Nature is invisible. In the same way, Mary went unnoticed in Nazareth. Because she was totally natural she did not stand out. Mary fit in because she was simply and wholly who she was created to be. Because she was perfectly natural, she was perfectly ordinary. Therefore, she was both as marvelous and as unremarkable as a morning in May. Meeting Mary may have been like seeing that Raphael Madonna. On the surface, it is a charming picture of a Mother and child. Look more closely and those who have eyes to see may just glimpse the magnitude and the mystery of God becoming man through the womb of a woman. Likewise, meeting Mary may have been like meeting any other woman, and only those with the vision of a mystic would have sensed the extraordinary truth expressed in this ordinary girl. This secret lies at the heart of Mary's purity, and it is this purity which makes her both invisible and invincible. Like a spy who "sleeps" in an enemy land, Mary fit in. This simple naturalness is the secret of her purity, which proves such a powerful secret weapon against the pride of the world.

Locked in that small Cowper Madonna is the natural innocence of Mary, and this simple innocence enabled her to be submissive to God's will. This is the little point of the fulcrum on which the world turns, and it is the point at which we can turn our world upside down. Can you see the revolutionary principle locked in this young woman's decision to be submissive to God? In our day, we howl at the mere idea that we ought to submit to anyone, and to suggest that a *woman* do so...it makes one a heretic ripe for burning. But let us stand that on its head. We assume that it is natural to be willful and to assert ourselves, but if there is a creator, then surely the natural thing is for all things to fit into their proper place in the natural order. To do this, one must find one's rightful place in that order, and submit to it. Therefore, if Mary was as natural and innocent as a morning in May, then she must have been submissive to God, because submission to God is the natural, wholesome and ordinary state for a human being. It is pride and self-will that are strange and twisted—not submission.

Therefore, a person who is submissive to God's will is natural—as natural as the sun which submits to rise and set each day or the water which submits to run down-hill. Because she was pure and natural, Mary was already where she should be. She didn't need to assert herself. She didn't need to establish her own identity. It was already solidly fixed in who she was. When she said to God, "Let it be done to me according to your word," she was saying something natural and ordinary because it is natural for a human being to submit to his maker. At the same time, it was strange and unexpected, because from the dawn of time human pride had come to seem natural, and rebellion against God had become the norm.

Thus Mary's response was revolutionary; for in a world of rebels, the one who submits is subversive. Mary's total acceptance of God's will turns the world upside down and points to a new way forward for humanity: a way in which purity replaces pride. This kind of purity is actually power, since it tunes its own small voice in perfect harmony with the vast crescendo summoned by the universe's conductor. Mary's pure submission to the Divine Will points to possibilities for us. If we align ourselves to the greatest power that exists, we become its agents in the world in ways we could never expect. To say "Thy will be done," therefore, is an exercise both in weakness and ultimate power. In admitting our lack of power, we open the door to God's. When Mary heard the words, "With God nothing is impossible," she plunged into a concept with everlasting, portentous potential. She embraced the exciting and frightening reality that she lived in an open

73

universe, a universe where it is possible to align oneself with a Will that is forever surprising and subversive—a Will that is itself a magnificent and mighty blend of purity and power.

C.S. Lewis observed that at the end there will only be two kinds of people—those who say, "Thy will be done" and those who say "My will be done." With Eve we may choose "my" or with Mary we may choose "thy." As it was in Eden, so it was in Nazareth, and as it was then, is now and ever shall be. We have a choice between our will or God's will. We can choose all that is twisted and tiny and tainted—or all that is natural, enormous and innocent. Like Eve and like Mary, we have been given free will. We can choose freedom or we can use that free will to choose slavery. We can limit ourselves to our own ever-narrowing will and so choose a downward spiral of impurity and impotence, or we can align our will to the Divine Will and be caught up in an upward spiral of purity and power that has no boundaries and no natural end.

CHAPTER SEVEN

Agony and Agnosticism

...he suffered under Pontius Pilate...

NOBODY SEEMS TO think about the suffering of Pontius Pilate himself. Pontius Pilate could be the portrait of the uncommitted man. Stuck in a job he probably doesn't like, he thinks he ought to "play the game" and "get ahead in life." So after sucking up to his superiors, he has been promoted beyond his abilities. He doesn't have the guts and gumption either to do his job well or to quit and go off to do what he really wants, like start a vineyard or breed horses, become a shopkeeper or learn to paint.

Pilate is one who passes his life in a state of "quiet desperation"—conforming to the system and doing his job, he is never able to commit to anything worthwhile, and is destined to spin his wheels. His inability to make a decision means he has no cause, no belief, nothing he'd die for, and therefore nothing to live for. He is the hollow man—

one of the vast anonymous mediocre millions who never do anything great, not because they are incapable or ungifted, but because they are paralyzed by their fear of what others might think—their deathly fear of making a mistake.

So he stands there helpless, trying to please the baying crowd, trying to please his pleading wife, trying to please his emperor, trying to please everyone, if only it were possible. Without belief in truth he has no conscience to rely on. Without belief in truth he has nowhere to turn, no resources for decision making, no foundation and no courage of his convictions—whatever *those* might be.

As one man he reveals all men who are incapacitated by agnosticism, emasculated by a maelstrom of contradictions, and deafened by the cacophony of confusing philosophies. He doesn't know where to turn, and like a child who sees he has lost a game, decides to quit. He simply washes his hands of it all and turns away, and in that refusal of choice he makes his fatal decision.

I nominate Pontius Pilate as patron saint of post-modernism. Like us, he lived in a sophisticated, multicultural society where different world religions jostled for attention and claimed to be right. Pilate was a politician who had to balance the fanatical demands of the Jews with the practical demands of the Romans. He comes across as a sincere, mediocre middle manager who wanted to please both the boss and the employees. Up to a point, Pilate respected the Jews. He probably thought all religions had some goodness and truth to them. They were all paths up the same mountain, and each person had to choose the one that worked best one for him. In other words, Pilate was a practical agnostic. His agnosticism seemed urbane, tolerant and practical, but his urbanity proved cruel, his tolerance allowed judicial murder and his practicality boiled to cowardice.

But if Pilate was a coward, he was also curious. No doubt he was sincere when he asked Christ, "What is truth?" Pilate understood that truth is a slippery thing, and that while every man has some of the truth, no one has it all. He may have been one of those who think the "spirit of inquiry" is more important than truth. He may have had a poster on his wall with a path leading into the distance and the motto, "To travel hopefully is better than to arrive." Pilate asked "What is truth?" but would not see that the One who called himself Truth was standing right in front of him. Because of this blissful blindness, Pontius Pilate is the model post-modernist. His blend of weary curiosity, cynicism, and careless agnosticism renders him, really, just a highly sophisticated man from Missouri. His famous appeal to the opinion of the mob is identical to the tyranny of the mob in our society—whether it is through the ballot box or so-called "market forces." Pilate's agnosticism is a sign of our times, but so is his agony. In a memorable play, Pontius Pilate is pictured in exile in his old age, still agonizing over his decision, or rather, his lack of a one. At that point Pilate realizes that his worst choice was that he made no choice.

Because Pilate could not see the Truth when it stood in front of him, we sadly admit in the creed that Jesus Christ "suffered under Pontius Pilate." Jesus Christ not only suffered by being tortured and killed, he suffered while he stood there waiting for a verdict. It is easy to forget that people suffer from indecision as much as from bad decision. We wish to view Jesus Christ from a safe, dispassionate distance—as we would any other historical figure. But Christ will not be treated like Abraham Lincoln or Mahatma Gandhi or Martin Luther King, Jr. His life and his legacy are far more demanding. Of all historical figures, the evidence on Jesus Christ demands a verdict. He says plainly, "Follow me" and "He who is not with me is against me."

Jesus Christ also said, "You cannot serve two masters." Being masterless was not an option. (Or, in Bob Dylan's words, "You gotta serve somebody.") Pilate's dilemma was indicative of our own. He wanted to wash his hands of Christ and get on with his career. But Pilate's choice was starker than he imagined. It was not between his career and Christ, but between Caligula and Christ. When Christ stood before him, Pilate was the servant of the emperor Tiberius, but waiting in the wings to step into his wicked uncle's big boots was the one known as little boots—or "Caligula." Just a few years after Christ was crucified, Caligula became emperor. While the story of how Christ rose from the dead began to circulate among the slaves of the empire, the psychopathic Caligula rose

78

to tyrannical power. The legends tell us that when the bad, mad teenager took the throne, Pilate was disgraced and sent into exile, where he eventually committed suicide. Pilate's story is a parable for all practical agnostics. The grim moral of the story is that you cannot avoid a choice. By not choosing, you are choosing. As for Pilate, the choice is between the master of this world or the master of the world to come. You must choose between Christ and Caligula, between the divine and the demonic, the god-man or the madman.

Pilate chose Caligula instead of Christ, but in an ironic quirk of history, both Christ and Caligula claimed to be an incarnate god. Jesus said, "I am Truth." Caligula said, "I am Zeus." Wasn't Pilate right to avoid such madness? Like Pilate, the sensible soul from Missouri wants to avoid all such extreme claims. It became clear that Caligula was a madman, but the disturbing thing about Christ is that while he made a mad-sounding claim, he still seems one of the sanest people ever to walk the earth. As we judge Caligula, we must judge Christ—by words and actions. When we do, Christ shines as the most whole (and hence the most holy) person who ever lived. Jesus does not claim to speak the truth as any good teacher may do. Instead he claims to be the Truth. This is the claim that demands a decision. If it is false, then he is a dangerous egomaniac and can be dismissed or locked up. If he is indeed the Truth, then he demands our total allegiance and the service of our whole life.

Pilate's response in the face of this person is the response most of us make. We wish to sit on the fence. We withhold judgment. We refer it to a majority vote so we don't have to take responsibility. This kind of agnosticism has a kind of ecstasy, taking us out of ourselves, not into the truth but into the tribe. Ignoring is bliss. But the hound of heaven sniffs us out, and our sloth turns from ecstasy to agony.

The greatest questions of life demand an answer, as a lover demands a commitment. Christianity, like life, demands that we make decisions. It demands that we use our will. It demands involvement. It does not take long to see that not to choose is, in itself, a choice. When a bus comes along, you can choose to get on the bus or stay on the bench. There is no middle option. You may quite fairly say that you do not know if the bus is going to the right destination, and choose to wait for the next one, but that too is a choice not to get on the bus. You may quite fairly say that you are uncertain as to the safety claims of the bus company and that you are withholding judgment for the time being, but that too is a choice not to get on the bus. According to the nature of choice, therefore, agnosticism is an illusion. It is wishful thinking. Like Pilate washing his hands of the whole matter, it is simply a stage gesture—an act that convinces only the actor.

The honest agnostic may come back with the reply, "I simply don't know." But what is it that he doesn't know that believers know? If he has explored religion and the claims of Jesus Christ, then he has as much knowledge about the Christian faith as most people do, and many people decide to set out on the adventure of faith based on that limited knowledge. Therefore, when the agnostic pleads that he "doesn't know" if there is a God or if Jesus Christ is the Savior of the World, he is simply admitting what all good Christians would admit to as well. Neither do they know for sure that there is a God and that Jesus is his Son.

There are different kinds of knowing. I knew enough about my wife to get married. I now know far more about her and she (to her chagrin) knows far more about me. In the marriage commitment comes a new kind of knowing which cannot be had on the other side of marriage. Within marriage there is a kind of human sacrifice. (That's why we say a person is being "led to the altar." In this mutual sacrifice of commitment, one enters into a new and frightening kind of knowledge, and it is the same with religious faith. There is plenty of astounding evidence, but always a leap of faith is required. One can take skydiving lessons, study aerodynamics, learn how to fold a parachute, and enter an airplane. One can don a helmet and a parachute, and stand at the door, but still one cannot know what skydiving is like. There comes a point when you have to jump.

Faith is a terrible and exciting gamble. Living by it means submitting yourself to a purpose. It means getting off the fence. It means getting up from the seat and saying "Let's roll!" By contrast, timid agnosticism seems so very safe. But its seeming safety is a berth on a sinking ship. Faith jumps for the life raft and swims for safety, or drowns in the attempt. It is no coincidence that the arch-agnostic Pontius Pilate committed suicide, for agnosticism insists that we cannot know if there is something worth living for, and if there is nothing, then why go on?

The life of faith, on the other hand, is a come-hell-or-high water adventure. It is true that some religious people have turned the life of faith into a secure and dull regime. They have frozen faith into a system which they treat like a spectator sport. It is as if they mistake watching ski jumping on television for actually putting on skis and taking off down the ramp. But the dullness of their religion cannot cancel the vibrant fact of faith. All those couch potatoes watching the ski jump on TV do not negate the people really jumping—or the real chance to live rather than watch others live.

Christ contrasts with Caligula, and Pilate with Simon Peter. Pilate washed his hands in a ceremony of detachment. Peter cries out to Jesus, "Do not wash just my head, but wash me all over!" Pilate is dispassionate while Peter is almost purple. Pilate seems wise in his detached deference to reason; Peter rashly plays the fool time and time again. Consider how Peter steps out of the boat on a stormy night to take the walk of faith. He rocks and reels as he walks on the water, then he finally starts to sink. Like Pilate, the detached agnostic remains safely in the boat and decides to ride out the storm. Like Peter, the person of faith steps out and walks forward into a world as uncertain as waves and wind—a world that opens onto perplexing possibilities. While faith too often ossifies into ritual and rules, in itself faith is that quality of life which surges within us and urges us to step out of the safe little boat and approach the edge of chaos. Faith takes us into the unknown, and at that point our tiny lives teeter on the brink of destruction, and on the brink of a life which is perpetually expanding into unimagined dimensions.

CHAPTER EIGHT

I Scream, Therefore I Am

...was crucified, died and was buried...

I LIKE A LINE in a Leonard Cohen poem, "There is a crack in everything. That's how the light gets in." The crack in the entire universe is pain and suffering. Stop for a moment. I am not mouthing the greeting card platitudes that say, "Every cloud has a silver lining" or "Bluebirds sing beyond the rainbow." I'm not reciting the mantra of the self-help experts who tell you that when the going gets tough, the tough get going, since they see that the glass is half full and not half empty. All these comforting and encouraging words may be true in their own way, but I am digging for a more deeply buried diamond.

The quest starts at the fault line running through the very genetic code of creation. There's a crack in the cosmos. There's a flaw in the foundations. There's a stain running through the warp and woof of the fabric of the universe. This crack is how the light gets in. What seemed to be the unutterable darkness turns out to be the shadow in the masterwork. It's like the artist who takes a brush and splashes the finished work with spots of paint; then when the light comes up you realize it was the speckled, dappled splatters of paint which give the whole piece texture and depth and a new kind of reality.

And so you whisper, "Glory be to God for dappled things," (Hopkins) because something clicks. A transaction takes place that you scarcely understand, and you realize that all the candied perfection was fake because it did not have the dark stain of suffering running through it. It's the authentic suffering of the world, not the artificial perfection we strive for, which brings us face to face with reality. Then you whisper again T.S. Eliot's admission that "human kind cannot bear very much reality," and this makes you pause and ponder the nature of reality in the first place: what is real and what is phony, and whether you are ephemeral and artificial, or authentic and lasting, and whether or not you have cracks, whether you leak or not, and if and when you see that you do have cracks—very fragile and deep fissures in your soul—you ask how they might possibly be where the light gets in.

When my nephew Michael was getting ready for college, he told me he was expected to write a paper in his first week entitled, "How do I know I exist?" After discussing the matter for some time, he concluded that the best thing to do was to punch his professor in the nose. The resulting pain when the professor punched back would thereby prove that both of them existed.

Michael was unusual for a college freshman. He was actually interested in the idea. Like anyone who has wondered if things continue to be there once you stop looking at them, Michael realized that in some way the existence of everything was linked with his own, and if he didn't exist, then maybe nothing else did either. To get some answers, he'd been snooping through some basic philosophy books and came across René Descartes' memorable sound byte, "I think therefore I am." Michael found it unconvincing, but wasn't sure why. Here's why: Descartes thought the fact that he was aware of the activity of his mind was the proof of his existence. For Descartes, thinking was not just a matter of logic or figuring out his tax return. It included the whole range of mental activity, like emotions and the experience of pleasure and pain. Despite all his doubts and uncertainty, he was at least certain that he was thinking, and that made him conclude that he existed. But the activity of our own mind is not a reliable proof for our existence for one simple reason: it is only the activity of our own mind. And so it might still all be an illusion; or as the scientist from Missouri might say, "just a series of chemical reactions."

To make sure we exist, we have to be in certain touch with something that really does exist outside ourselves. But can the existence of the external, physical world prove our own existence? Not really, because we perceive the external world through our senses, which in turn are filtered through our mind. In other words, we perceive everything outside ourselves with our brain—which is inside ourselves. Therefore, it is difficult to prove that there is really anything outside ourselves at all. The skeptic's reaction to the supernatural is "It's only in your head." But if you follow the philosopher from Missouri far enough, you will discover that everything else is, too. And if everything is "only in your head," then you yourself are "only in your head," and whether you really exist or not is an open question. If this is true, then "I think, therefore I am" should be rephrased as, "I think, therefore I think I am" or "I think, therefore I think I might be." In other words, Descartes was because he thought, but he was not what he thought he was.

Is there anything outside ourselves with which we can make contact to validate our existence? What about that lift of the mind and heart when I view a beautiful person, a Raphael Madonna or a breath-taking landscape? Does the experience of aesthetic pleasure prove I exist? It certainly hints at something greater than ourselves, but pleasure is notoriously fickle. What pleases one may sicken another. At times, pleasure may point us toward an objective existence outside ourselves, but that process is unreliable because it is often unrepeatable. So we return to that same mountain top to experience that same sunset which was so sublime, and all we see is the sun disappearing below the hills, so we decide to sit down and eat a sandwich. Finally, the man from Missouri will also point out that what we experience as pleasure is also just a series of chemical reactions. So if our senses and our experience of pleasure cannot validate our existence, what can?

Fed up with such pointless speculation, Dr. Johnson famously kicked a stone to prove that he was real. But what was it about kicking the stone that convinced Dr. Johnson that he existed? Would he have been as convinced if he had kissed the stone and not kicked it? I doubt it. It was not only the solidity of the stone, but also the nerve endings in his toes that convinced him that he and the stone both existed. In other words, pain proves our existence. As he hops around on one foot, Dr. Johnson tops Descartes with a new proof of human existence. Between his gasps of pain he might have also gasped, "I scream, therefore I am!"

Could it be that pain is the ultimate proof of our existence? The man from Missouri will step in at this point to remind us that pain, too, is merely a sensation of the brain and therefore just a chemical reaction. But pain is different from the other sensations that the brain interprets. First of all, pain is the most intense sensation of all. We know that pleasure feels good, but we *really* know pain feels bad. Even the most pleasurable experience is not as good as having a tooth pulled out is bad.

Secondly, sensory information and the experience of pleasure are mixed with a mass of data in our brains which causes us to interpret the sensations in subtle and subjective ways, and this process permits all sorts of unreliable conclusions. So, for instance, the physical pleasure of being kissed is mixed with our feelings for the person doing the kissing, our moral framework and the complexity of sexual arousal. All of this complicates and confuses the simple pleasure of kissing. Pain, on the other hand, is simple, raw data. Pain is not subtle. It is sharply negative and cannot be either ignored or misinterpreted. Even a masochist winces before he sighs.

Have you noticed how pain is typically surprising? This leads to the conclusion that it is an authentic experience, because we would not be surprised by something which we'd devised or desired for ourselves. Therefore pain validates my own experience because it clearly comes from outside myself. My desire for pleasure or information leads me to pursue pleasurable and interesting stimuli, but that pleasure and information cannot prove my existence because I pursued it, and because I pursued it, I was biased. In contrast, pain is an interloper. It is something I do not seek. It is a shock that invades my life. Pain is therefore the most accurate proof of our existence, a little morsel of objective truth. That "truth hurts" is true in far deeper ways than we thought.

Pain also validates our existence because, unlike pleasure, it is not fickle. Different brains treat pleasurable stimuli in different ways. The sunset that gives you pleasure may cause me to yawn. The opera that I find thrilling, you will find killing. I like broccoli raw, but you can only eat it with cheese sauce. Taste makes pleasure subjective and ephemeral, but when all of us kick a stone, all of us dance with pain and thus prove our existence. Similarly, the effect of pain is repeatable. When you go to see a sunset again you may not get the same sensation, but when you kick the stone again you will experience the same sensation every time. Thus pain is the most reliable, fixed and authentic proof of our existence.

Pleasure anesthetizes the soul, but pain is the pinch that wakes us up. What makes us face the largest and most dangerous questions of life? Sometimes pleasure, but more often pain. Someone is diagnosed with cancer, or we cling to the precipice of life after an accident, or a car knocks down our child. Then, in the terror and tremendous pain, we know beyond a shadow of a doubt that we exist. There, in the screaming darkness, we understand that we are alive even if we wish we were dead.

Pain proves our existence in a negative way. It screams out to us that something is missing. Something is wrong. Things are not as they should be. Pain is very powerful, but it is not positive. It is real, but it is not reality. Pain is like a shadow. As a shadow proves the existence of the object that casts the shadow, so pain proves we are really here. But a shadow also proves the existence of light. The light is the positive quality that, by default, produces the shadow. Likewise pain, because it is negative, tells us not only that we exist, but that there must be such a thing as an existence without pain. In the same way, hunger and thirst not only prove the existence of our stomach, but they demand the existence of food and drink.

If all this is true, then my nephew's conclusion that he should punch his professor in the nose was deeply meaningful. The point of the professor's bloody nose is that suffering is actually our most authentic human experience. I think, therefore I am? No. I scream, therefore I am. Once this proposition is put into the context of Christian belief, it becomes apparent why Jesus Christ is called a "man of sorrows and acquainted with grief." (Is. 53:3) If God was going to take human form, and if the most acute and authentic human experience is pain, then it makes sense that the god-man would have intense pain at the very core of his experience.

This is why Catholics have crucifixes in all their churches: because they prove that we all exist. The climax of Jesus Christ's human existence was the excruciating reality of crucifixion. Not only was Jesus Christ's crucifixion physically painful, but it was psychologically tormenting. At the cross, a person everyone admitted was good and wise was killed as a criminal. So the suffering seemed senseless. It was absurd, and this is surely the most terrible thing about suffering. No one objects too much when a wicked person dies a long and painful death, but when a little child is abused, we react with incoherent fury. In the face of such absurd horror, we shake our fist and ask "Why?" But there is no answer. The evil was absurd and meaningless. That's why it's evil. That's why it hurts. And it is at this point of cosmic anguish that all humanity is most achingly alive.

Suffering is not only the proof of our existence, it is the turning point of the whole drama of why we are here at all. In the face of innocent suffering, Jesus Christ did not deliver a neat philosophical discourse. He did not expound a spiritual method that would provide an escape route. Instead in a most awesome, tragic and dramatic action, Christ embraced suffering and went through it. This is what we mean when we say that his death was redemptive. It is not so much that he redeemed us, but that he introduced the possibility that suffering itself could be a redemptive transaction. He did this not with words, but action. He accepted his sentence and went to an absurd, agonizing and humiliating death. Then at the darkest moment he proclaimed the most eloquent and moving sermon on suffering ever preached, by crying, "It is finished!"

When examining any religion, one must examine how it deals with this problem of suffering. By his example on the cross, Christ shows us the authentic Christian way. Buddhism seeks to overcome suffering and rise above it. Primitive religions offer sacrifices to gods who promise to deliver the devotee from suffering. Indeed, certain forms of Christianity also make this false promise. But they are wrong. Jesus Christ showed a new way. To be authentically human, to be really alive, to know we exist most fully, we have to scream. We have to go through suffering—not around it or over it. That's what he meant when he said, "If any man would be my disciple he must take up his cross and follow me."

Jesus realized that to be authentically human, we cannot avoid suffering. Doesn't the fact that we came into the world howling and will leave it whimpering suggest the same grim truth? Suffering is at the core of our existence. We cannot put it on to someone else as a scapegoat. Instead we have to face it. We have to go through the surgery of suffering in order to be healed. Jesus suffers and dies not to deliver us out of suffering, but to deliver us through suffering. He shows us that the only way to cope with suffering is to wrestle with it and pull a reversal. Christianity calls us to win a victory, not run from the fight.

The Christian life is not about picking spiritual posies and feeling happy in Jesus. It is about establishing a mysterious bond with this most mysterious of men. It means linking ourselves to Jesus Christ—who wrestled alone with the demon of suffering. In a strange and symbiotic relationship, the Christian claims to plunge into the stark reality of Christ's crucifixion. He does this through the mysterious rituals of religion, and through the mundane rituals of his own human suffering. In that crushing process the ordinary Christian begins to find redemption and release. This "salvation" Christians talk about is therefore not a season ticket on the bus to heaven. It is a summons to battle and the invitation to risk all to share in the chance of victory over evil.

Salvation as the final holiday in heaven has made of Christianity sentimental, irrelevant nonsense. Many sensible people rightly reject such a greeting-card religion. They perceive it as an escape route from reality, when in fact it is an expressway straight into the heart of things. It is true that many Christians use their creed as a cozy cop out, but for every hundred who do, there are ten like Mother Teresa or the old pastor in the ghetto who realize that at the heart of Christianity is the stark fact of the crucifixion of Jesus Christ. That absurd torture at the core of the Christian faith forces them to confront the reality of human existence. As these authentic Christians take on the burden of suffering, they enter a new dimension of human reality—a dimension where everything is as hard and beautiful as diamonds, a dimension where they find divine power hidden in frailty and a tender humility that sweats glory.

CHAPTER NINE

Out of the Frying Pan Into the Fire

...He descended into hell...

IT IS A MARK OF man's perversity that he is always striving to go up. He makes airplanes and rockets that can never go high enough. He wants to be promoted. He wants to be top of the class, head of the company and A-Number-One in all things. Do you see how unnatural this is? In the world of nature things go down, not up. Water flows downhill. Heavy things sink. Only that which is light and insubstantial rises up. Trees grow up, but only after first putting their roots down deep.

That which is humble and natural and true, therefore, goes down, not up—or at least it goes down first. The humble and meek will be exalted, and the rich and powerful will be put down. It is the way the world works. It's one of the rules of the universe. If it is true that what is natural goes down before it goes up, then that which is most natural must be the One who invented nature and that One is God himself. Thus an old Jewish proverb says, "We must go down to meet God for he is always below us." Here is something strange; we always thought God was "up there." It now appears that God is actually "down here." It turns out he is not only large, but also little. Not only is he "down here," but part of his very nature, like all of nature, is to go down, not up.

This little truth is locked into the creed at this point. When we say Christ "descended into hell," we're saying he went down—way down deep into not just the netherworld, but the world beyond the netherworld, the deep darkness of the abyss, the emptiness of the valley of the shadow of death, the nothing: "the unimaginable zero summer (T.S. Eliot)." This descent into the dark is fundamental and foundational, and what it actually means and where he actually went require that we descend as well, for it is a law of the cosmos that we must go down if we ever hope to go up.

Someone once asked the famous mystic Padre Pio what he thought of modern people who didn't believe in hell. His terse reply was, "They will believe in hell when they get there."

Is it possible to believe in hell? Surely, when faced with Auschwitz, Hiroshima, the Gulag and the killing fields, the question should be, "Is it possible not to believe in hell?" I don't simply refer to the fact that concentration camps were a kind of hell on earth. Instead I wonder how one can deny the existence of a place of severe punishment when faced with Adolph Hitler, Joseph Stalin, Pol Pot, Idi Amin and African soldiers who chop off little girls' hands for fun. When faced with such monsters, can we really cry with a good conscience, "God would not send anyone to burn forever in the fires of everlasting torment!" After a century that has witnessed more genocide, religious martyrdom and brutality to children than ever before in human history, can we really dismiss the only punishment left for the dictators, abortionists, terrorist bombers and genocidal maniacs who have got away with their crimes? If it were true that there is no hell, I, for one, would be howling with rage at the insanity and unfairness of it all. Yet those who deny the existence of hell calmly assume that their denial shows how enlightened and humane (and therefore fair) they are.

These are good people. They dismiss the possibility of hell not because they deny the wickedness of human beings, but because they affirm the goodness of God. They believe in a God who is so very good that he would not send anyone to hell. It would certainly be nice if there were a heaven but not a hell. But can you believe in one without the other? What I mean is, how can someone believe in heaven, which must after all, be a place of goodness (and if goodness, then justice), while denying the fact of hell which makes justice possible? Therefore it seems to me, that if you believe in heaven you must also believe in hell. Hell is somehow written into the constitution of heaven.

Nevertheless, good-hearted people insist that a good God would not possibly send anyone to be tormented in hell for all eternity. This is a laudable sentiment, but I worry that that's all it is: a sentiment. Nevertheless, the conviction that God would could not send anyone to hell is a feeling I myself incline to—especially after a warm day in May followed by a very good dinner with four glasses of claret. Furthermore, at that moment I am not usually thinking about Pol Pot or Stalin. I am thinking that God would not send an ordinary, decent fellow like myself to hell.

But this is exactly the point where the possibility of hell is meant to knock me down and shake me up. We are told that the road to hell is a wide smooth, downhill highway, while the road to heaven is a narrow and hard mountainous climb. What if hell were populated with hordes of overweight, complacent people just like me, who never really did anything magnificently evil, but also never bothered to do anything spectacularly good? Why should we imagine that heaven is reserved for the mediocre?

When I look at it this way, I have the dreadful suspicion that perhaps those who deny hell because God is too good to send anyone there are really proposing that God is too good to send *them* there. It is ironic that people who believe in heaven are sometimes blamed for wishful thinking. Isn't it that more likely true of those who disbelieve in hell? I say this because the person who disbelieves in hell doesn't really believe in heaven either. He believes in oblivion. He desperately hopes that he will cease to exist after death. In other words, he hopes he will get away with it after all, and this, it seems to me, is real wishful thinking.

Others protest that the concept of eternal punishment makes God out to be an angry, short-tempered disciplinarian of the worst sort. But is God such a nice middle-class English gentleman that he would not be angry enough to send anyone to hell? What if God were more like a passionate and hot-tempered Mediterranean papa? That is not to say that God is petulant and petty. He isn't angry with wickedness the same way our fifteen-year old is angry, and therefore refuses to tidy his room. God does not slam the door and stamp his foot. Neither is God angry the way we are when we don't get our way. He does not sulk, dish the ice, and then pretend nothing is wrong. If God is angry with the wicked, it is not because he is an arbitrary and babyish tyrant who loses his temper when is disobeyed.

What if, instead, God's anger is the sort we feel when we hear of a young boy being abducted, raped, killed, and chucked into a ditch? What if God's anger is the sort of anger and revulsion you feel when you see a young African woman whose hands have been cut off by rampaging soldiers, and who cannot cuddle the child those same soldiers gave her when they raped her? What if

God's anger is the disgust you feel when you hear of a dowager who leaves her vast estate to her poodles, in a world of starving children? When you hear such news don't you respond with an element of rage as well as disbelief, horror and grief? Aren't you righteous to do so? Perhaps God is angry at the wicked in the same way. He sees the everlasting beauty of goodness, the vibrant potential of each human being and the stunning radiance of his creation, and when it is soiled, trampled, raped and chucked into a ditch by humanity's folly, greed, stupidity and violence, God is full of fury, frustration, sorrow and compassion.

Does that mean God would cast someone down into hell to be tortured forever? Perhaps this, too, can be seen the other way around. Is God too good to send someone to hell? It could be that God is so good that he actually gives everyone exactly what he or she wants. If we have spent our whole lives pursuing love, goodness, beauty and truth, then after death we may get exactly what we always wanted and find ourselves in a land where love, goodness, beauty and truth are as natural and abundant as light. On the other hand, if our whole lives are spent in an insane flight from all that is good, beautiful and true, then perhaps God in his goodness will also give us exactly what we always wanted; that would be existence in a madhouse with no exit, where love, beauty, goodness and truth were unknown: an existence in the outer darkness with gibbering maniacs like ourselves.

Life pans out, and despite our greatest efforts, we almost always end up getting what we really want. In fact, this sort of justice is built into the system. We will get what we want, just as naturally and certainly as an acorn becomes an oak tree. Giving people what they really want is natural justice. To do otherwise would be cruel. We think everyone ought to go to heaven, but can we imagine that a person who hated God, goodness, truth and beauty all his life would actually enjoy heaven? If they could visit that place of eternal beauty and laughter, they would howl with serious terror and run with all their might in the other direction. We know this is true because there are people in this life who hate truth, beauty, and goodness and do everything in their power to flee from the light.

Is hell a real place? Now, this is where the topic really starts to interest me. I find it interesting because, down through the ages, human beings from every culture and time have recorded fascinating stories about their visits to hell. I wish I could recount them all, because they are far more fun and interesting than philosophical speculation on the topic. Here is one story: The philosopher A.J. Ayer (who was a noted rationalist and atheist) choked on a piece of smoked salmon and "died." His heart stopped for four minutes before he was revived. Once he came back he recounted his experience. His biographer writes, "He had been confronted by a bright red light, painful even when he turned away from it, which he understood to be responsible for the government of the universe.... Ayer became more and more desperate...when he regained consciousness he spoke about crossing a river—presumably the river Styx—which he claimed to have crossed." In subsequent interviews Ayer admitted that the experience had made him feel "wobbly," but he soon reverted to type and labeled himself as a "born-again atheist."

Witches, exorcists and mediums tell us how they have summoned or wrestled against the inhabitants of hell. The famous sixteenth-century magician John Dee summoned a demon and described him thus, "He appeared in his red apparell: & he opened his Clothes & there did issue, mighty & most terrible gastly Flames of Fire out of his sides: which no mortall eye could abide to looke upon any long while. And in the marvelous raging Fire, the word BRORGES did appeare tossed to and from in the fiery flames."

The visionaries at Fatima were given glimpses of demons and hell as well. One of them described the sight,

> The rays of light seemed to penetrate the earth, and we saw, as it were, a sea of fire. Plunged in this fire were demons and souls in human form, like transparent burning embers, all blackened or burnished bronze floating about in the conflagration, now raised into the air by the flames that issued from within themselves together with great clouds of smoke, now falling back on every side like sparks in huge fires, without

weight or equilibrium, amid shrieks and groans of pain and despair…the demons could be distinguished by their terrifying and repellent likeness to frightful and unknown animals, black and transparent like burning coals.

Now for my money, this is real religion. It makes my blood race with excitement. This is jalapeño faith—green hot, mouth-and-eye-watering religion. Literally hot stuff. These are the sort of outrageous religious experiences you want to bring up in that circle of educated and urbane religious folks just to see their politely horrified reaction. Don't you think that a real creed ought to feature juicy bits like this? In fact, it could almost be the test of a substantial faith that it has ecstatic visions and horrifying encounters with the supernatural. I don't say that proves a religion true, but it renders it real, and any creed that weeds out such stuff due to good taste or fashionable incredulity is not a religion at all, but a set of table manners.

These visions of hell and devils don't make for happy bedtime reading—especially if your bed happens to be a deathbed. Despite my delight with such visions, I realize that such things don't constitute proof for the existence of hell. On the other hand, if hell is a "real place" in some sense, how else would we be able to experience it, except through visions, dreams and almost dying?

We are inclined to dismiss near-death experiences and mystical visions as "bad dreams." But what do we know about dreams? Doesn't psychology suggest that our dreams provide an interface with the daemonic realm? We say such a realm is not real, and argue that the physical world is the only "real" one, and yet modern physics deals with strange parallel dimensions of reality all the time. The world of sub-atomic particles is both "real" and "unreal," depending on your point of view. Is there any reason why what we call the spiritual dimension might not also be real according to its own terms of reference? What if the human mind is the final frontier, and dreams, visions and near-death experiences are precisely the way we gain access to this other realm?

We are treading in the twilight zone here, but let us suppose that mystical visions, dreams and near-death experiences are a kind of travel to a foreign land. Maybe instead of giving us visions of their own fantasies, the magicians, visionaries and nearly dead really are giving us a glimpse of another dimension of reality. If they are, then it matches up with a universal strain in human consciousness, for practically every religion and culture perpetuates similar stories of human visitors who return from the underworld with horrific tales of justice for the wicked. The person who denies hell is therefore the outsider, the renegade and the strange one—not the soul who affirms it.

Those who disbelieve in hell will say that the case is not proven. This argument is like one of those tetherball games—knock the ball away from you and it swings around to hit you on the head. So if reports that hell exists don't prove it exists, then fervent denials do not prove that it doesn't. The question remains open, and if it remains open, then I know which way I would wager. Suddenly, believing in heaven and hell is not wishful thinking at all. It is prudent—as prudent as a second parachute or a life insurance policy.

The Christian position on hell is quite plain—to the point of being impolite. The Christian preacher delivers a simple two-word sermon on the subject: "Fear hell." I realize this may be too crude for those of delicate religious sensibilities. Some will complain that such sermons get people into heaven only by scaring them out of hell. There are certainly more noble reasons for desiring heaven, but none more effective. I admit that I am human. I am scared of monsters, demons and death, pitchforks, and pain, and if there is such a place as heaven and hell, I, for one, would rather be scared into heaven than soothed into hell. Is my vision of heaven and hell too literal? Once again, I would rather learn secondhand one day that my vision of hell was too literal than find out for myself it wasn't literal enough.

If such a place exists, I naturally wonder what Jesus Christ was doing there. Perhaps if his mission was to go down, he had to go all the way down. Perhaps this answers the question of how a good God can allow people to choose hell. He only does because he was prepared to go there himself and rescue them. Certainly the tradition is that once he died on the cross, Jesus descended into the underworld like Orpheus to find and rescue his loved ones. This poignant possibility is put most simply by a child who was receiving religious instruction. The priest asked the question, "Where did Jesus go after he had died on the cross?" The little boy sat and pondered the question for some time. Eventually, he put his face in his hands. Finally, he looked up with an expression of great sorrow on his face, and said with great solemnity, "I think he went down to the deepest darkest corner of hell to look for his friend Judas."

If this is so, then perhaps the notion of Christ descending into hell indicates a regular habit of his. Could it be that while his justice cannot obliterate hell, his mercy provides an everlasting redemption from its torment? Every prisoner hopes for reprieve, and every convicted criminal hopes for pardon. Can such hope be in vain? Can there be such a thing as thirst if there is no water? Maybe that phrase "he descended into hell" can be stretched to suppose that forever Christ is reaching down into hell, and that until the end of time he will be throwing down a lifeline—hoping that someone down there might just give it a tug.

CHAPTER TEN

Memes, Magicians and Manichees

...On the third day he rose again...

FOR THOSE (LIKE ME) who live in a world of words and a universe of abstract ideas, it is often difficult to connect with what we call the physical realm. Chances are, if you are reading this book, that you are one of those mentally astute but physically inept type of people. You prefer to think first and take action later (if then). Theoretically you *can* change the oil in the car, but it's a hot and dirty chore. You'll scrape your knuckles and knock your head and swear and come up greasy and then realize you've left the wrench in the crankometer (or some such). Yes, yes, in theory you *could* drill the holes and put up those shelves your spouse has asked you to fix for the last three years, but you know you will be impatient and hasty. You'll cut the wood at the wrong angle, pockmark the wall with drilled holes and then watch with horror as the books are put on the shelves and they teeter and lean and totter before crashing to the ground.

These painful experiences of the physicality of life are the wake-up call reminding you that all is not abstract thought, beautiful ideas, profound philosophy and intriguing theories. So it is with the Resurrection of Jesus Christ. Here the theology and philosophy stop, and historical, gritty, physical truth begins. Here the abstract theories become concrete realities. Here humanity is forced to reckon with an event that, if it is true, changes everything. This is why, in every age and at every place for the last two thousand years, Christians have circled their life around a day in the Spring called "Easter."

On this day, they stop to take account of all things. They spot-check their apprehension of reality. They halt to put their world in a proper perspective and to order their lives according to a fact of history that must be reckoned with. It is this astonishing fact that jolts us out of our penchant for philosophy, the paralysis of analysis, our abstract thought and our lofty theories, and makes us gasp and rearrange ourselves, our thoughts, our lives, our loves, our everything.

Some years ago there was an Anglican bishop who was asked his opinion about the Christian belief that Jesus Christ rose from the dead on the third day. The bishop said he believed in the resurrection, but not in any crude physical way. "The resurrection," he stated, "was not a conjuring trick with bones." What many people did not notice at the time was that this was a conjuring trick with words. The bishop, like many modern theologians, was an expert at verbal legerdemain. What the bishop meant was that he believed in the resurrection, but not the physical resurrection. This is like saying, "I believe in marriage, but not a marriage where people do anything so crude as to make love."

Many modern clergymen and women understand the resurrection in this way. Like most magicians, they use this sleight of hand to mystify and entertain their audience. So on Easter Day, Reverend Mandrake will stand in the pulpit and proclaim, "Today we celebrate the glorious resurrection of Our Lord Jesus Christ from the dead." What he means by this is, "In some wonderful way the teachings of Jesus were remembered by his disciples after he was dead." However, what Mrs. Bloggins in the front row thinks he means is that he believes that Jesus' body was brought back to life miraculously, that his disciples saw it, put their fingers in the nail holes, and watched him eat a breakfast of broiled fish and toast. With this verbal trick Reverend Mandrake is able to please both Mrs. Bloggins and the bishop. In other words he is able to fool everybody—even himself.

A plain-thinking person might be excused for distrusting the clergyman, and for thinking, "He has said one thing, but means another!" It is then understandable when the

ordinary fellow in the street puts the modern clergyman in
the same category as the politician, the used-car salesman
and the snake-oil man. It is easy to criticize this clergyman
for being dishonest, but we must forgive him. Like the naked emperor's courtiers, he has only believed what he has
been told to believe. Furthermore, the modernist bishop
and his clergy sincerely believe that by saying one thing and
meaning another in this way, they are being more honest.
So the bishop might say, "I am not so naïve or literal in my
understanding as to expect Jesus to physically rise from
the dead. Surely the true meaning of this belief is that he
continued to exist in some spiritual manner."

The problem is the old either/or dilemma. Those who
deny the physical resurrection in favor of a spiritual meaning assume that those who believe in the physical must be
so dumbly awe-struck by the miracle, that they miss its
spiritual meaning. This is a mistake. The joy of believing
in the physical resurrection is that you can believe in the
spiritual meaning too. In fact, the latter entirely depends
upon the former. It is the physical fact of the resurrection that makes the spiritual aspect jump up and dance a
jig. In the same way, my marriage has spiritual meaning
through my wife and I making love. You could say that it
is only because a husband and wife make love that they
understand love.

Anyway, aren't you suspicious of any theory that is
all "spiritual"? It is too ethereal and otherworldly. Any
religion which "spiritualizes" away the physical aspect

indicates a negative attitude towards the physical side of life. This negativity towards anything physical was made famous by a third century thinker called Mani. His followers were called Manichees, which makes them sound like a cross between a sea cow and a Chinese fruit. Despite the difficult name, they taught something that is very easy to believe: that the physical is filthy, vulgar and nasty, while the spiritual is clean, ethereal and nice. But I am suspicious of things that are so easy to believe. They make us all too comfortable and they don't have the smell of truth.

Mani concluded that the physical was inferior because he thought that Satan had stolen particles of light from the world of Light and imprisoned them in man's brain. The object of religion was to liberate these particles of light from their sordid physical captivity. The way to release the light imprisoned in the brain was to beat down the body by means of extreme asceticism. I doubt that the Anglican bishop I mentioned was a Manichee in the respect that he went in for whips and fasting. The man I have in mind was plump, and somewhat of a bon vivant. I can hardly imagine him sacrificing his dining rights at high table to sit in a snowdrift in his underpants in order to liberate the particles of light from his brain. However, inasmuch as he found the physical resurrection of Jesus to be distasteful, he was indeed a Manichee.

I use the word "distasteful" because I suspect that educated and sophisticated people deny physical miracles not so much because they are incredible, but because they are *tacky*. It is true that physical miracles are embarrassing. There is something mad, subversive and unpredictable about miracles, and I wonder whether intellectuals deny them simply for this reason. However, one's fear of being embarrassed is itself a shameful thing to admit, so they devise intellectual reasons for not believing in the miraculous. The most famous foundation for this denial is the philosophy of David Hume, who said that miracles are impossible because they defy the laws of nature—and hence, in the case of any report of a miracle, it is much more likely the witness is lying or deluded than that those immutable laws had been suspended. This allegedly watertight philosophical conclusion seems pretty leaky to me.

Doesn't it all depend on your prior assumptions? Hume assumed that the physical universe ran like a clock, according to fixed and unalterable principles. Therefore, miracles were impossible. If something seemed to be miraculous, it was simply because we hadn't yet figured out how it fit into the machine of the cosmos. But if the universe is actually expanding, as we now think, doesn't that indicate that it is not quite so fixed as we thought? Perhaps the cosmos is more like rubber than concrete. If that is so, then the unpredictable is possible, and strange things can happen. If the universe is elastic, then rather than miracles being an aberration from the natural order, they might well be an ordinary but unpredictable part of it. To look at it another way, the universe might be more like a party than a stage play.

Perhaps then, God is a God of surprises, a God who likes tricks, twists in the tail, paradoxes, and unexpected pleasures. Miracles, and especially the resurrection of Jesus Christ, are just that sort of reversal we would expect from a good storyteller. The hero descends to the darkest depth, and at that point he turns the plot, twists the knife, and rises to triumph. Now this historical, physical miracle carries enormous spiritual significance, but if you deny its grounding in earthy, material truth, haven't you made it a non-event? It's a sign that points to nothing real, after all. And doesn't that render it, really, *insignificant*?

Saying you believe in the resurrection only in "a spiritual sense" is not to believe in the resurrection at all, because the whole astounding and scandalous point of the resurrection is that it was physical. Two thousand years ago, hundreds of witnesses reported seeing a man alive whom three days before they had seen being tortured to death. The witnesses reported being frightened out of their wits. They thought it was an apparition or a ghost, but then they saw him eat fish and bread. They touched him and put their fingers in his oozing wounds.

This is not what happens when something is true "in a spiritual sense." When something is true "in a spiritual sense," bishops discuss it with their clergy over a glass of dry sherry. When something is true "in a spiritual sense," old ladies of both genders mutter together around crystal balls and packs of Tarot cards. When something is true "in a spiritual sense," people sit with their legs crossed and hum Hindi words together. But when something like the resurrection is true, really, utterly and physically true, then people are scared. They run and weep and cry out in fear. Then, once they have grasped the reality of the event, they get on and do something. They do not do something "in a spiritual sense," they do something real and physical and world changing.

This is precisely what happened after the resurrection of Jesus Christ. Eleven working-class men who were hiding for fear of their lives suddenly became the nucleus of a force that changed the world forever. Something must have happened, and it was not simply that "in some wonderful spiritual way, the teachings of their friends continued to echo in their minds and spread around the world." This theory reminds me of a fascinating idea of Professor Dawkins. He suggests that there is such a thing as a "meme." A "meme" is a piece of information that reproduces much like a gene, spreading from one brain to another. Through the mechanism of memes, dead people can seem to live in a vivid way decades later, and their ideas may spread after they die. This is an interesting concept, and some people have found it a beautiful way to think of Jesus Christ's resurrection.

But the resurrection of Jesus Christ from the dead is far more than either a memory or a meme. Those of us who believe, freely admit that the event is embarrassingly vulgar. We think it *really* happened. We believe it is a physical, historical and actual fact like the assassination of JFK or the coronation of Queen Elizabeth. Furthermore, some of us are delighted to believe that there is a photograph of the actual moment. We theorize that the darkness of the tomb acted like the inside of a camera, and the radiance of that resurrection burnt Jesus' physical features into the inside of his shroud, and that you can see the Polaroid snapshot of the event to this day in the cathedral in Turin. If the scientist tells us it is twelve hundred years out of date, we reply, "Maybe the radiation from the burst of energy that caused the resurrection threw the carbon dating out of whack. Isn't that what you would expect from a God of surprises? He's keeping you guessing, after all; there's got to be some room left for faith."

Of course, the resurrection is an astounding miracle. It is a totally unique event, but then, that is the definition of a miracle—it is an unpredictable blip in the normal day-to-day running of things. From an everyday point of view, the resurrection seems incredible, but if you accept the primary doctrine of the Christian faith—that Jesus is God in human form—then the resurrection is not so surprising at all. If he really is a totally unique synthesis of divinity and humanity, wouldn't you expect something unique to happen when he died? If he really is the god-man, would you expect him to stay dead?

Belief in the physical resurrection is actually crucial to the whole Christian faith, because Christianity is about the reality and possibility of a new kind of human existence. Jesus rose from the dead simply because there was nothing dead about him. In other words, because there was nothing decaying and impure about him, he could not stay dead. His life was so dynamic, vital and pure, that it simply had to come back again. It could not be killed forever. Instead, it bursts from the darkness of death with a life that is not less real, but more real than what we had come to expect. The resurrection of Jesus Christ comes trumpeting in with its sheer, unexpected and blatant physicality—not as something unnatural, but more natural than we could have imagined. His resurrection says, "What you thought was life is a pallid reflection of life. See this resurrection body? This is what life is. It is not death. Real life cannot die."

Furthermore, he said this is why he came: "to give life in all its abundance." This doesn't simply mean he comes to give everyone a happy life, it means he comes to give life itself—which by definition is the opposite of death. He offers this life to all those who wish to accept it. It is a gift, and like any gift, it must be either accepted or rejected. To ignore it is a way of rejecting the gift. Turning this fact into a "spiritual" truth is also a way of rejecting it. It is a very subtle and refined rejection—like accepting a gift, then keeping the greeting card, and tossing the package itself in the trash.

Emasculating the resurrection by turning it into a "spiritual truth" won't do, any more than ravenous teens could be made to settle for "spiritual pizza." By its own definition, the resurrection is a historical, physical event, and the documents of the early Church are written to express exactly this unpalatable and socially awkward fact. This is why the first Christian theologian said in a most astringent manner, "If the resurrection did not happen, then our faith is in vain." In other words, "If this isn't true, then the rest of it isn't either. Let's not mince words and go all gooey and spiritual. Either it happened, or it didn't. Billions of people for the last two thousand years believe it did happen. If you've examined the evidence, and you think this astounding miracle really took place in a backwater of the Roman Empire around the year 33AD, then follow the logic and become a Christian. If you don't believe it, then eat, drink and be merry, for tomorrow you die. But please don't spiritualize the whole thing. That is not one of the options. Mystic pizza is not on the menu."

CHAPTER ELEVEN

Somewhere Over the Rainbow

...He ascended into heaven...

WE SAY, "WHAT goes up must come down," but if that which goes up must come down, then according to the divine cosmic principles (which stand all expectations on their head) then what comes down must go up. That is to say that what is lowly will be exalted, and what is humble will be lifted high. Just as the greatest (according to the divine economy) must come down, so the lowest must rise up.

This suddenly throws new perspective on a quite ancient story. It shifts our paradigm and shows us reality in a new way. When we think of Jesus Christ rising from the tomb, we understand that it is not so strange after all. It is simply the way things work in that other realm. We see that, for him, resurrection is part of the natural/ supernatural order of being. He went down into death.

That means he must rise up into life. It's as natural as water flowing downhill, but also as natural as water being evaporated. What went down must go up. God came down to take the form of a human being. Therefore, he must rise up again into the heavenly realm. It's as simple as a sunrise. What goes up must come down? No. What comes down must go up.

It is this topsy-turvy view of reality which the Ascension of Christ introduces. Just as the Ascension reverses the laws of gravity, so it flips all the expectations we had of reality. Here we say a *resurrected person went up to heaven*, and we are supposed to believe it really happened. There is something radical and revolutionary to this. It should be seismic in its alteration of our perceptions of reality, and yet we yawn and scratch and wonder what is for lunch.

The Ascension introduces us to a frightening and delightful new perspective of what we consider "reality," and we don't have the eyes to see it. We're blinded by familiarity with a religious story which we've seen in stained-glass windows and illustrated Sunday-School books, when what we are faced with is an altered perception that should be as disconcerting as one of those episodes of *The Twilight Zone* that kept us awake and pondering.

Those who like *The Twilight Zone* and fairy tales should love the story of the Ascension of Jesus Christ into heaven. Like Dorothy, who is swept up by a cyclone to Oz, Jesus floats up and disappears up into what must be a Technicolor heaven. Fantasy tales are full of this sort of thing. Peter Pan flies away to Neverland, Mary Poppins is whisked away when the wind changes, and the space ship comes to carry E.T. home to his peaceful planet.

It is easy enough to dismiss the Ascension story as a piece of first-century science fiction. Jesus had to go somewhere after he rose from the dead, so the first-century Isaac Asimov said, "I know—let's beam him up. Sounds cool." But it has the awful whiff of a *deus ex machina*, except in reverse. In ancient plays, the god was cranked down onto the stage to resolve the plot and bring a happy ending. Here, the God is cranked up from the stage to disappear in a cloud of glory and live happily ever after. We can almost see the scenery shudder and catch a glimpse of the dry-ice machine. It is easy enough to see the similarities of the Ascension to fairy tales, sci-fi movies and Broadway shows, and we assume that since the fairy stories are untrue, then the Ascension is also untrue. But what if it is the other way around? We think the Ascension story is untrue because we have heard similar stories that we know are fantasy. But if the Ascension actually happened as it was reported, then it might be a kind of fulfillment of the other stories, the history that made all those fictions in some sense true.

Think, for example, of all the fantasy stories about princesses marrying handsome princes despite all the odds. When a real girl finds true love and marries the man of her dreams, does she not make all the fantasy stories come true? When the man is transformed by her radiant and faithful love from a slavering primate into a civilized husband and father, have the couple not made all the Beauty-and-the-Beast stories come true?

In a similar way, when a hero really does, in a unique incident, ascend into heaven, he validates all those stories where the hero rises up and flies away home. But for this to be true we must imagine just how such an implausible story might have actually played out.

Can we even begin to believe that Jesus Christ was "beamed up" into heaven? It depends on your point of view. Not long ago, the news reported the first steps being taken towards teleportation. Can we be so credulous as to really accept that Jesus floated up into the air and disappeared from sight? Why not? Levitation is well documented in the annals of mysticism. In fact, it is one of the more common and most reliably witnessed of the supernatural phenomena. Lots of people saw St. Teresa of Avila levitate, and St. Joseph Cupertino was so adept at levitation that he was eventually named patron saint of pilots and airline hostesses. Levitation is not even that impressive amongst believers. When that scientist, Thomas Aquinas, was summoned to witness the remarkable case of a nun who could float, he simply remarked, "I didn't know nuns wore such big boots." Mystics of other religions have also been observed to defy the normal laws of gravity: fakirs float, poltergeists make heavy objects fly through the air, and the demon-possessed are known to both roar and soar.

I point this out not to say that the Ascension was simply a case of teleportation or levitation, but to embarrass the empiricists among us. The empiricist says he will only believe something that can be seen with his own eyes or verified by credible eyewitnesses. Then when credible eyewitnesses report that a saint has levitated or that they have seen a demon-possessed person thrown across the room by some malevolent force, the empiricist denies that it happened. So he doesn't believe eyewitnesses after all. He believes his prejudices. When St. Thomas Aquinas saw the levitating nun, he also saw the joke, and that's one of the delightful things about levitation stories. The Ascension is much more important than a simple case of levitation, but the same sense of *joie de vivre* is there, and the Ascension, like levitation, reminds us that the law of gravity is sometimes broken by levity.

So if gravity is sometimes defied in a supernatural way, how might this make us reconsider the Ascension of Jesus Christ from the earth? The account given in the New Testament says he floated up into the clouds, and eventually faded from sight. This is more than levitation. He didn't just go up and come down. He went up, then he disappeared. This sounds unbelievable, but isn't this what we would expect if someone were to be taken physically from the material realm into the spiritual realm? Even if we think this is where Jesus went, the whole story sounds as if "going to the spiritual realm" means that he became less physical. Most of us have this annoying tendency to spiritualize such stories and make them ghostly, ethereal and weird. But what if it is the other way around? What if Jesus did not become less physical, but more? What if he vanished into another realm that is not less real, but more?

How can this be? Am I simply spinning theories and being fanciful? No. I'm serious, and as usual, everything depends on our starting point of view. We naturally assume that this physical world is the real, solid and substantial realm, while the spiritual realm is ethereal, wispy, transparent and therefore less real. But who is to say which is more real—the invisible realm or the visible? Most people think the world of spirits is ethereal while the physical world is solid; but what if it is exactly the other way around? Let's imagine Aunt Susan said she saw an angel pass through a brick wall. We would assume that the angel was ethereal and "unreal" because we assume the brick wall is solid. But what if angels are more solid and eternal than brick walls? If they are, then it is the wall that is flimsy and insubstantial.

How do we know which one passed through the other? Physics tells us that what we consider solid matter is mostly empty space. What if the angels (whom we think of as creatures of air) are, in fact, made of some matter more dense and solid than the brick wall? Then the angel may have passed through the brick wall as a man passes through a bank of fog. If you didn't know the nature of fog or a human being, and you witnessed a man step through a bank of fog, wouldn't it be easy to believe that he was ethereal and the fog was solid?

Can we rely on our perceptions to tell us what is real and unreal? The physicists tell us that material reality behaves in very strange and contradictory ways, and the physicians tell us that our senses are very easily fooled. If the physical world is more fickle than we thought, and if our eyes and ears cannot always be trusted, perhaps the more trustworthy world is the one that transcends all senses. Saint Paul agrees with Plato that the invisible things are more permanent than the visible. If this is the case, then the person who believes in the reality of the spiritual dimension may be more of a realist than the man from Missouri. Similarly, if this whole material world is compacted from dust, air and water, and if it will eventually return to dust and ash, then the stout materialist is the one who trusts in the ephemeral.

So, in the Ascension, it could be that while the disciples "saw" Jesus vaporize into the spiritual realm, he in fact passed through a "cloud of fog" into a realm that is realer than ours. From his point of view, he was leaving the fuzzy, unstable world behind and entering one that is far more stable, colorful, vibrant and alive than this world. What if all the lurid religious art, with its ghastly colors and vivid detail, points to some reality we hadn't counted on? What if heaven is as bright, colorful and flamboyant as a Mardi Gras parade, an amusement park or a Hindu festival? If this is so, then when Jesus went from this world to the next, he was simply leaving a vague shadow world to step into a world where the light is like crystal and each grain of dust is as hard and beautiful as diamonds.

If this is so, then the story of the Ascension teaches us several things about the relationship between the spiritual world and the physical. First of all, there is commerce between the two. Plato thought that spiritual beings were able to assume physical forms. But if their world is more real, then for them to take a physical form would require them to slow down and dim their energy. Or, if you like, for these beings to become physical is to wade through a world that is thick and cumbersome, dark and cold. For them to take human form would be like one of us wading through icy molasses up to our neck.

But if the door between the worlds is open, and spiritual beings are able to make themselves visible in physical form, it would follow that after death, human beings might be able to enter that spiritual realm. However, humans are physical beings. Physicality is an intrinsic part of our nature. Our bodies aren't shells for our souls. They are an indivisible part of our souls. Therefore, human beings must enter the spiritual realm in some physical sense. They don't become angels or ghosts; instead, their physicalness becomes spiritualized. It is not done away with, it is transformed to a higher plane of material reality. If this is so, then the Ascension shows this very process happening. Jesus didn't just become a disembodied spirit. He didn't turn into a ghost, he became a spiritualized physical being.

The Ascension was a unique event because it was a first in human history. When Jesus was "taken up into heaven," what really happened was that the door swung open for physical humanity to be divinized. By this action, the physical was actually brought into heaven, and a physical dimension was introduced to the spiritual realm.

That is why St. Paul insists (despite the contradictions and seeming absurdities) that when we die and are resurrected, we shall have what he calls a "resurrection body." The actual physical components will not be reconstituted from dust and ash, but the physical dimension to our souls will live on. It is difficult to imagine this without imagining that we shall be like ghosts. Turn that on its head by imagining that what we are now is ghostly compared to what we shall be. Those "resurrection bodies" we are promised will be more real, more youthful, more eternal and more beautiful than we can ever imagine; they will be so much more real than these bodies, that they will be to these bodies as a real landscape is to a black-and-white photograph.

Do we have trouble imagining such things? I don't know why. We accept the miracles of technology every day, but if someone had told our grandparents that we could feed a piece of paper into a machine in Peru which would then turn it into a series of bleeps which were transmitted millions of miles to a little machine spinning in space, only to bounce back to another machine in Pennsylvania, which then printed the image onto another piece of paper, they would think we were dangerously mad dreamers. If we told our grandparents that a machine the size of a notebook would transmit the text of a book from California to Karachi in the time it takes me to blink, they would ridicule such fantasies.

So why can we not imagine that similarly "unbelievable" things might be possible in that last frontier—the one between the physical and the spiritual realms? The person of faith stands on the edge of these possibilities and has room to muse, room to surmise, and room to theorize. Anything is possible, after all, and it is up to our imagination to try to visualize what it all means and what kind of world is on the other side. Suddenly the person of faith is not an antique leftover of a bygone age, but the dreamer on the cutting edge. Suddenly it is the dull empiricist who seems like the Luddite, the Mennonite and the antiquarian.

The Ascension simply tells me that it the world is open-ended, and that I can expect the unexpected. In fact, *it might happen to me*. I can be transformed; I can have commerce with the spiritual world. I can make contact, and one day make that same journey from what seems to be real to a reality that is more hard and glorious than I could ever imagine. Furthermore, that reality is not some dreamy ectoplasmic existence. It is firm and real and delightful. Do we think that these physical bodies give us pleasure? We haven't yet experienced pleasure. What we have had here is merely a glimpse of the glory that is to come. The most exquisite music here is only a whisper of the music of that greater reality. When you begin to catch a glimpse of this other country, the ancient words ring true. The heart lifts to think that it really may be so that eye has not seen, nor ear heard, nor the heart of man conceived of such glories that await us.

CHAPTER TWELVE

Ambitiously Ambidextrous

...and is seated at the right hand of the Father...

THERE ARE FEW things easier to forget in the daily run of life than the enigmatic oxymoron that I am both an enigma and a moron. That is to say, I am both an angel and an ape. I am Beauty and the Beast. I am Body and Soul. I am mortal dust and immortal diamond. I am made of mud and stars, earth and air, manure and fire. The problem is that, too often, I do not behave like the hybrid I am, but I am one moment a Beauty and the next moment a Beast. I am, in a moment of prayer, an angel, and the next, in a moment of exasperation, an ape. I try to puzzle out this strange and marvelous truth and cannot come up with a solution to the conundrum.

All I can do is explain what I am not: I am not a soul trapped in a body, the way a genie might be trapped in a lamp. My body is not simply a vehicle from which my soul will escape once I have reached my destination. Neither is my soul in my body as water is in a sponge. Do I think that through death, the sponge will be squeezed, and my soul will drip out? No, I am a mysterious union of body and soul. So perhaps my soul relates to my body as a wick is in a candle—as the flame burns the wax melts and merges with the wick, and the candle and wick become one and are consumed. In all of these images, the soul is considered somehow superior to the body and so all of these images are faulty; we must not believe that the body, simply because it is prone to decay, is inferior to the soul.

Instead, there must be some other, more mysterious and inexplicable relationship between our souls and our bodies. We think of them as two, but they are meant to be one. We think of death as the separation of soul and body, but perhaps the end point of all our spiritual quest and our physical life is that the two do not separate, but become one in a more mysterious way than we can imagine. The idea that Christ "sits at the right hand of the Father" might just introduce us to a newer, stranger way of perceiving this reality—one that astounds and confounds all that we thought before.

Some time ago, I heard an Oxford theologian being quizzed on the radio about a book he had just written on God. The interviewer was doing his best to trivialize the topic in order to appeal to his audience and consolidate their secular mindset. He chided the theologian for being credulous. How could he possibly believe in such an outmoded and superstitious thing as the Christian creed? How could an intelligent modern philosopher believe in such fairy-tale stuff as angels, miracles, and Jesus sitting on a throne at God's right hand in glory? How could he be so literal?

The theologian politely replied that he didn't really believe God had a "right hand" or that Jesus sat on a throne in the sky. This was, he explained, a turn of phrase to express the spiritual truth that Jesus was given a place of spiritual power. If he had been given more time, the theologian would have gone on to explain that God is pure Spirit. He has no body. He is the Divine Essence, the Supreme Intelligence, the Uncaused Cause and the Being Beyond all Being. God is the Unimaginable One. In fact, God is so completely beyond human imagination, that as soon as we say something about God we must turn around and say that what we have said is not really true.

This way of knowing by not knowing is called the apophatic way, which always sounds to me like a rather nasty digestive problem. However, this particular Oxford theologian sounded better than most of his breed, and I'm sure he is right to tell us that God is pure Spirit and beyond all our knowing. But the problem with this way of talking about God is that he very quickly becomes less than what we expect him to be, rather than more. When we say, "Everything we think about God is not true," we should be acknowledging that what we have said is insufficient. In other words, God is bigger than what we can think, not smaller. Of course God is greater than anything we can think or say about him, but when we become too pessimistic about our ability to say anything true about God, it is not long before we come to believe that there *is* nothing true about God. In other words, if we say nothing about him he soon turns out to be nothing.

Eventually, I began to take the side of the terrier-like radio man. I wished he had challenged the theologian a bit more and not allowed him to duck into the nearest metaphor for cover. It sounds good to say, "God doesn't have a right hand and Jesus doesn't sit on a throne in heaven," but how do we know Jesus doesn't sit on a throne, and that God doesn't have a right hand? If heaven is brighter and bolder, more tangible and physical than we thought, maybe God is too, and if he is, then perhaps he is physical in some way beyond our wildest imagination. This detail began to trouble me. What if God is physical in some way? What if he does have a right hand? It seems ridiculous to suggest such a thing, but why not give it a try? After all, I am standing on my head; why not try it on a tightrope, just for fun?

Of course God cannot be physical the way we are physical. For us, the material world is locked into the realm of time and space, and this means that everything material is subject to change, death and decay. So God can't be physical like that. He doesn't go around checking his watch or worrying about either deadlines or wrinkle lines. However, if we insist that God is Pure Spirit and not physical in any sense, aren't we dismissing the physical as being ultimately unimportant? After all, one of the quirkiest and most unexpected lessons from the Old Testament is that we humans are made in God's image and likeness. But we aren't purely spiritual beings. We are hybrids. We are flesh/spirit beings—creatures of earth and air. We are inspired mud. This means our bodies are a vitally integral part of us. Our bodies are not simply a husk for our souls. We are not soul-filled bodies, we are embodied souls. Our souls permeate every aspect of our bodies. Therefore, our bodies matter, and if we are made in God's image, then surely our bodies, too, must be part of that image. So I began to wonder if God didn't have some sort of body after all, and if a body, then a right hand.

Furthermore, the Christian church teaches that this Supreme Being actually took on physical form in the person of Jesus Christ. If God took a human body, then what seems a strange action to us must have been natural to him. In other words, he took the form of something he already was. God cannot turn into something he isn't. He doesn't transmogrify. Therefore, if he assumed the form of a human being in a particular place and time, then in some sense he must have had that form already, outside of place and time. By now I had worked myself into a little state of excited heresy. It was a genuine puzzle. To my mind, God had to have a body, but I knew it couldn't be so because everyone said it wasn't.

But why not stand this received wisdom on its head? Why shouldn't God, in some unimaginable way, have a physical dimension? We have a problem with this because we continue to imagine that the physical is inferior to the spiritual. But what if the fullness of reality is to be both physical and spiritual? There is an old Islamic legend which says that Satan was furious with jealousy when God created humans because they were physical and spiritual beings, while he was only spiritual. The implication is that the little human beasts were actually superior to Satan because, having bodies as well as spirits, they were more like God. We deny that God has a physical dimension because, for us, whatever is physical must be subject to limitations, and we know God cannot be limited by anything. We say God is not physical because we cannot imagine a material existence that exists outside space and time. But what if there was actually a kind of physicalness that existed in a dynamic, yet unchanging way, outside space and time? Indeed, in those moments when we are struck by beauty, don't we get a tiny glimpse of immortality, and isn't that everlasting quality linked with the physical beauty we perceive? At that moment in front of the Raphael Madonna, or before the beloved, don't we get the very impression that we are on the edge of a vast reality that is not less real, but more real than we could have imagined? Isn't part of that impression the feeling that there is a kind of physical beauty and reality that transcends the limitations of time and space?

The core belief of the Christian faith makes this outrageous suggestion seem even more probable. If God really did take human flesh in Jesus Christ, and if that flesh was brought back to life and taken up into heaven, then through that action, there is a physical dimension woven into the Being of God. This is where the phrase "seated at the right hand of the Father" starts to get interesting. The story of the Ascension indicates that Jesus went up into heaven in bodily form. He did not become a ghost. His body did not disintegrate. Instead, his physical form was somehow transposed into a new dimension of reality. By this action he must have done something stupendous—he must have integrated human physicalness into the Being of God. In other words, Jesus is not only the image of God here on earth, but he is the image of God in heaven as well. Of course, being God, that physical quality cannot change or be limited to one place and time. Instead the physical image of man in God exists like a dynamic, yet static, icon at the heart of the Godhead.

If there is a physical dimension to God, then because it is physical, it must move, because anything that is physical and alive must move in some way. Otherwise, it is just a picture, a corpse or a statue of the physical. But if this God moves, it cannot change. This is what Christians are hinting at when they speak of the Trinity being a unity of dynamic love. In God, three persons exist in one Unified

Being. The spiritual aspect is the Father. The physical aspect is the Son. The mental aspect is the Holy Spirit. The three are in a constant dance of dynamic interaction while they are also in perfect harmony. This threefold unity spins like a top—in perfect motion, yet perfectly at rest. It is like a mighty waterfall—always in motion, always the same, and never the same. Because the three persons are in a constant action between themselves, the "physical" aspect of God remains real, vital and eternal.

Another way of thinking of this is that the Son not only sits at the right hand of the father, but he is the right hand of the father. At one point Jesus himself said that what he did was by the "finger of God." So if he is the finger he might just as well be the right hand, and if he is the right hand of God, then the third person of the Trinity—the Holy Spirit, could be the left hand. So if God is three equal persons in one, and one person in three, that makes God ambitiously ambidextrous. As a result, God clapping his hands with joy and delight at creation might be one of the best images of the Trinity we can come up with. Likewise, when the children sing, "He's got the whole world in his hands," they might be singing the glories of the greatest mystery of them all—the mystery of the most holy, glorious and undivided Trinity.

So perhaps the doctrine of the Trinity reveals a God who does have, in an unimaginable way, a physical and a spiritual aspect that are totally intertwined. The two aspects are united as they exist in an endlessly intricate and fascinating relationship. If this is true in heaven, then it is true on earth. Don't I know myself to be most physical and most spiritual when I am in a relationship of love or hatred with someone else? On my own, I may descend to a state of simple brutish physicality and extinguish the spirit, or I may purse a solitary and ascetic life, and become a "spiritual" being. However, when I am making love or punching someone in the nose or laughing at a joke or listening to a bore or sharing a pint of beer with a friend, I am most alive as a human being. And that means I am most fully and unselfconsciously alive in a physical and spiritual way at the same time.

This is why people get married, join a club, play football, go to the theater and join a church: so they can be in relationship with others, and be more alive than they can be in any other way. Whenever we get together in a relationship there is a physical and spiritual element at work—even if it is at work in a degraded and degrading manner. But when Christians go to church, the two elements of the physical and spiritual are explicitly brought together. At church, they do something spiritual through a physical action: they join the body of Christ by getting dunked in a tank of water. They renew their membership by eating bread and drinking wine that has itself been transformed into something that is a supernatural union of the physical and spiritual.

Finally, if the truth that Jesus Christ is "seated at the right hand of the Father" indicates that somehow the physical is a part even of God himself, then suddenly the physical is important. More than ever, matter *matters*. If this is so, then what I do with this physical life of mine may turn out to be just as important as what I do with my spiritual life. If the two are intertwined, then they affect each other. This has been part of Christian teaching since time immemorial. With this body I may turn my soul towards hell, or with this body I may turn myself towards heaven. If this is the case, then the little physical things are important, and that is why Christ said God had numbered the hairs of our head, knows when a sparrow falls, and that we will be judged for every idle word spoken. In other words, because Jesus is seated at God's right hand, every little decision, word and action matters. If the little actions matter, then I may turn towards the outer darkness with an action as small as sneering at my neighbor, or I may I may start the long journey home with an action as small as getting down on my knees.

CHAPTER THIRTEEN

Myths, Movies and Medieval Cathedrals

*...He will come again to judge
the living and the dead...*

IF THERE IS SUCH a thing as truth, then it must be something, like air, that is at once outside myself and inside. If truth is only inside me, then it can only be understood by my own inner responses: what I think and what I feel— my thoughts and emotions. If what determines my truth is merely my own thoughts and emotions, then truth is fickle, because not only do my thoughts and emotions contradict those of other people, they often contradict themselves. So I sometimes think and feel that chastity and temperance and self control are good and other times I am just as convinced that lust and gluttony and drunkenness must be better.

Therefore, truth must be outside me as well as inside me. In other words, there has to be some greater standard for what is true (and therefore for what is right and wrong) than my own inner thoughts and emotions. I need some external standard to go by. Where could that external standard for what is true, what is beautiful, what is good and right originate? It must originate in a mind that is greater than mine.

If there is such a thing as external truth, then there is also such a thing as choice. I can choose to align my own 'truth' with The Truth. Or I can choose not to. This element of choice is at the heart of what we mean by "judgment." Judgment is choice, and when we say that Christ will come to judge the living and the dead, you could say he is coming to exercise his choice between who will live forever and who will die forever. How he makes that choice is what is intriguing. I, for one, think his choice is rather simple and surprising: he chooses what we have already chosen. He gives us what we want. His judgment confirms our own choices—and there's a fearful thought!

I like the movies. I don't go in for those sophisticated French films where men and women smoke cigarettes in bed and discuss the meaning of life in anguished whispers. Neither am I am fan of serious films with social messages. I like Hollywood pictures with big heroes, big villains and big explosions. I am a sucker for a well-crafted story, a good plot line, and a happy ending. Despite the complaints of both the puritans and the purists, popular movies are essentially good. That is to say, they are moral. In almost every movie, the bad guy loses and the good guy wins.

The cynic will observe that this is because the marketing men have figured out that the crowds like big villains, big heroes, and happy endings. This is probably true, but what interests me is why the crowds like happy endings, and what kind of happy endings they like. It is too simple to dismiss *hoi polloi* just because they like a "happy ending." They do not like happy endings per se, because they do not want a happy ending for everyone. They only want the good people to be happy. They want the bad people to be unhappy at the end. So in fact, the ordinary person doesn't like happy endings, he likes *just* endings. That's why ordinary people also enjoy a tragedy, because in a classical tragedy, a flawed hero gets what is coming to him, and what is coming is not a happy ending.

People have enjoyed drama with justice at the end ever since the first storyteller sat down beside the campfire. The search for meaning, and therefore for justice, has always been at the heart of storytelling. Through the great myths, ordinary people worked out the rules and guidelines of justice. Through the great stories, they told others how to live and what payment to expect for both their pains and their pleasures. Through myths and movies, ordinary people are reminded about good and evil and the final reward.

A sense of good and evil is universal to the human race. No matter what their culture, tribe, society or club, people understand that there is such a thing as right and wrong. They may disagree about the details, but nobody disputes that there is such a thing as right and wrong. In fact, because they argue about the question proves that they both agree there's an answer, one that is important enough to quarrel about.

Linked with this universal human instinct that there is right and wrong is the conviction that good will be rewarded and evil punished. The reason people like their movies, plays, myths and stories to provide justice is because there is so precious little of it in their ordinary lives. All around them, they see rich people getting richer and poor people getting poorer. They see that crime does pay, that cheaters do actually win, and that goodness doesn't seem to triumph. They know this isn't fair. They realize that justice in this life is a rare thing, and so they look to their movies, stories and myths to find a world that is fair. Because we have this unshakeable belief in the concept of right, wrong and justice, we demand that justice be done; we have a deep, unshakeable belief that one day things will be sorted out and complete justice will be delivered.

This might be dismissed as wishful thinking; what turns that upside down, though, is that while we all insist on justice, when justice arrives it is rarely what we have wished for. In other words, justice is usually not what we expect. To judge properly, we must have all the facts. To judge fairly, we must judge not only the action, but we must also weigh up all the extenuating circumstances, all the motives, and all the results of the action. As a result, there is only one person who can know all the facts, and that is the person who knows everything. The only person who knows everything is God, therefore the only possible judge also turns out to be the fairest possible judge. Indeed, based on those criteria, God is the only one who can give a totally fair, impartial and unbiased judgment. If this is true, then the Christian idea of a final judgment becomes not only a doctrine, but a desire. If we want justice and a fair hearing, as all sane people do, then the final judgment is not only something to fear, but something to hope for. Furthermore, while we may hope for justice, it is impossible (because we do not have all the facts) to know what form that justice will take. Therefore the only thing we can predict is that the final judgment will be unpredictable.

About fifteen years ago I visited the magnificent Cathedral of Chartres in France. At the time, an eccentric Englishman lived in a small apartment in the city, and dedicated his life to giving English-language tours of the cathedral. I happened to find myself on one of his famous excursions. Toward the end of our tramp around this most awesome temple to the incarnation of the Son of God, we wound up at the great South Door. Over the portal is a carving of the Last Judgment, with Christ seated on the judgment throne. Before him stands St. Michael with his scales of justice. On the right-hand side, the graves are being opened, and angels are assisting the righteous to rise to eternal life. On the left, grimacing demons are spearing the wicked and pushing them down into the everlasting fires. My overly vivid imagination warmed to this medieval scenario. It may have been devised in the "Dark Ages," but it didn't seem dark to me. On the contrary, the delicately carved scene, set like a jewel in the magnificent cathedral, seemed like a burst of radiant light in our own dark age.

The Englishman began his lecture by saying, "Notice that the judgment has to take place at the end of time, not at the end of our lives. That is because we will be judged not only by our decisions and deeds, but also by the effects of each decision and action, and of course, the effects of all our decisions and actions cannot be tallied until the end of time. The effects of each decision and action ripple outward forever down the centuries." This little aside struck me quite hard, and it hurt. It is quite disturbing to imagine that, not only will our actions, words and decisions be judged, but also every effect and consequence of our actions as they reverberate down through the ages.

Then the English aesthete caught my attention a second time. "Do notice," he said, "how the stone carver seven hundred years ago took the trouble to carve the faces on both sides with an expression of surprise." Indeed, when I looked closely, I saw he was right. Both the damned and the saved registered surprise at the outcome. This, in itself, is a surprising but sensible observation. Those who are destined for heaven are humble, and therefore they will be surprised because they do not think they deserve it. At the same time, those who are damned, being proud, are sure they don't merit hell. I was further delighted to see that among the damned were a couple of bishops and monks, while among the saved were women and men who, by their dress, had clearly lived for pleasure.

Such subversion of the social order is totally consistent with the Gospel stories. The one who turned over the tables in the temple overturned everyone's expectations. At the final judgment he will turn them over again. That the final judgment will be a surprise is one of those subversive details to which everyone ought to pay attention. If we believe there is meaning to life, then we must believe in justice, and if true justice considers and weighs up all the facts, then it must happen, as my English friend observed, at the end of time. Since this is so, there is naturally an awful lot of room for surprise. Who knows what evil may flow from that one bad, selfish and nasty decision of mine, which at the time seemed insignificant? What everlasting glory, on the other hand, might grow from one small act of kindness? At the same time, who can guess how a seemingly bad decision might be turned, by our shame, for the good; while a seemingly good action might be distorted into terrible evil by pride or perverted motives?

Time will tell. So, for example, consider the nameless stone carver at Chartres seven hundred years ago. Carving those faces was perhaps just another day's work. He did his best and was intelligent enough to understand why the faces should show surprise. He probably died as he lived—as a poor, unknown craftsman. Then one day, hundreds of years later, an eccentric Englishman noticed the detail and passed it on to countless pilgrims. I heard the story and have told many people, and now you are reading it in this book. Perhaps you will be inspired, and one day go out to change the world with a life on fire with goodness and love. And that humble stone carver in France so long ago will get some of the credit.

This is the surprising nature of providence, and why studying the way of God's will in the world is far more interesting than the most intricately woven plot of any drama, movie or novel. The tiniest seeds may grow into the greatest of trees, and that is part of what Christ meant when he preached about mustard seeds. The tiniest action may bring about the greatest result. Who would have imagined, for instance, that the political execution of a small-town street preacher in a backwater of the Roman Empire would redeem the world? This everlasting plot twist is one of the most fascinating and absorbing aspects of the last judgment. What a compelling idea, to imagine that every thought, word and deed will one day be counted and given its just and proper reward! Yet this certainty remains within the human heart. We know that the play will have a final act. Summer will draw to a close, the days will get shorter, the nights colder, and harvest will come.

There are those who deny this truth, but if anything is true, then the inescapable fact of judgment must also be true. What I mean is that for there to be such a thing as truth at all, then there must logically be such a thing as judgment, which is simply the final proclamation and clear resolution of truth. As St. Paul put it, "Now we see through a glass, darkly; but then face to face." In other words, the time must come when all falsehood fades away, all dissimulation, phoniness and presumption are revealed to be a cheap charade. Then the truth shall be told. All shall be revealed. What is secret shall be shouted from the housetops. This must happen simply because it is the very nature of truth to be proclaimed. Truth is something that has an inner, inexorable drive to be revealed. It cannot be concealed forever. Like the murderer's confession in Dostoevsky's *Crime and Punishment,* the grisly story cannot be suppressed. Truth will out.

If truth, like light, cannot finally be hidden, then lies have a built-in instability. They have a natural inclination to disintegrate, topple and fall. As a result there must come a time, if not in this life, then in the next, when all the paper pride, tinselly show and shallow trickery of deceit and self-deceit must be stripped away. Judgment Day is that time. For the medieval stone carver, this included Christ on his judgment seat, weighing up the good and evil we have done or not done, and this image is as good as any. After all, Jesus Christ claimed to be the Truth as well as the Way and the Life. Seeing him as he really is will be the very essence of judgment. In fact, why do we need anything else? To see him will be to reveal our whole lives for what they really were. In his light we shall see light. In his light we shall also see the darkness—perhaps for the first time—and for most people, a true vision of both the horror of the dark and the glory of the light will be judgment in itself.

At that point, all the choices we have made will be summarised by one choice. At that point, every knee shall bow and every tongue confess that Jesus Christ is Lord. After their initial surprise, some will confess his Lordship through gritted teeth, bowing the knee with terror and hatred in their hearts until the very end. To see him will be to see everything they have always hated and despised. To see him will be to acknowledge that they were wrong, very wrong, about everything. At that point, even the good they have done will be soured by their rebellion and become for them the desperate actions and decisions of the damned.

For others, the surprise will be just as great, but in seeing him they will see the Beauty they have always loved, the Truth they have always sought, and the Love they always knew existed. For those who, even unknowingly, have followed the light will be taken into the light. At that point, all their decisions and deeds will be redeemed. The redeemed will be surprised, because for them, nothing was wasted. Everything was gathered up, and even the sordid deeds and decisions will have been turned around. Their decisions and deeds, which were spotted with shadow, will be revealed as dappled glories. Their wrong turnings will prove to have been the scenic route, their failures will be revealed as learning points, and their battle scars will be their red badges of courage.

Because the judgment cannot come until the end of time, and because it will be full of surprises, we are told not to judge anything in this life. How can we ever analyze the mass of hidden motives? How can we negotiate the labyrinth of our hidden desires, our unconscious instincts, and the circumstances of our crimes? To embark upon that route is to be stuck down by the paralysis of analysis. That path is endless, dark and eternally confusing. It is right not to judge lest we be judged, and the sting in the tail of that saying is that if we do judge, then we shall be judged by the worst and most unfair judge of all: ourselves.

Better to throw ourselves on the Mercy. Better to trust the judge who knows all, since to know all is to forgive all. In the meantime, if we take such a view, we can live in freedom. As Christ teaches us, we can simply trust in God like little children (Matt. 18:3). We can live each day to the best of our ability and take no thought for tomorrow. We can look to the flowers of the field and the birds of the air and learn from them how to live. They do not toil, neither do they spin. They do not judge. If we can only cultivate that kind of simple trust, then when the end comes we might just awake from our sleep with a gasp of surprise and find ourselves being lifted up to a burning justice that has already been completed by mercy.

CHAPTER FOURTEEN

Nature's Bonfire, World's Wildfire

...I believe in the Holy Spirit...

THERE IS A POINT in C.S. Lewis' *Chronicles of Narnia* when the children are reminded that the great lion Aslan is "good" but is not "tame." It is a salubrious point which ought to be remembered when anyone speaks of the Holy Spirit.

We want the Holy Spirit to be a comforting glow, a kindly light, a warm presence or a peaceful feeling within. In other words, we want campfire Christianity. We forget that our God is a consuming fire, and that when we ask for the Holy Spirit, we may get a wildfire, a bonfire, a furnace, a burning bush or a stream of lava erupting from the depths. Aslan is not a tame lion. The Holy Spirit is not a candle flame, and the Holy Spirit (although he is a comforter) is not given to keep us comfortable. He comforts us the way the dentist does when he is drilling. "There, there, it will be all right in the end—but first I must drill and fill."

Because we sense this is true, we usually throw cold water to put the fire out. We disarm the threat. We calm the storm, we try to beat the heat, and there is no more effective way to do this than through religion. I am not referring here to real faith—the upsetting thunder-and-lightning, fire-and-earthquake creed, but polite, urbane and 'nice' religion—the sect of the well-to-do, the well-off, the well-spoken, the well-connected, the well-thought-of, and the well, just plain boring.

The Holy Spirit is our individual connection with the force of creation, the chthonic, underground fire that fuels the cosmos. It is the life of all things, funnelled into one person and ultimately into me. Its task is nothing less than transforming me into the immortal god-like creature that I was intended to be; at this terrifying prospect, I must stop and decide to either kneel or run.

When the Crown took a census in England a few years ago, there was a whimsical religious revolution led by *Star Wars* fans. They encouraged as many people as possible to write "Jedi" in the "what religion" space on their census form. This is the sort of subversive gesture I find entertaining, and, living in England at the time, I only resisted putting "Jedi" on my own form out of a conviction that the Christians needed all the help they could get. In fact, I had heard only a few months previously about one British *Star Wars* fan who watches the film every Sunday morning. I knew *Star Wars* was a cult movie, but I didn't know it had actually formed a cult.

But one has to look on the bright side. This might be the start of an exciting trend. It may be the way to get people back to church. Disenchanted clergymen looking for a new idea might install wide screens in their churches and beckon more of the *Star Wars* faithful to participate in the cosmic clash between good and evil each Sunday morning. With a bit of musical ingenuity, the *Star Wars* theme music could be developed into a very stirring processional hymn. Acolytes could be dressed in Obi Wan Kenobi monastic robes and carry light sabers instead of candles. The liturgy could begin with, "May the Force be with you." To which all reply, "And with your spirit." For the communion hymn, each Han could sing a solo.

The Jedi religion is a spoof, but the truth is oft spoken in jest. There is indeed a famine of real faith and potent myth in our postmodern culture. Talk of the Force may be the most theological discourse some people ever engage in. We shouldn't complain too much. The films might just remind the audience that there is a battle between good and evil going on, and that there are actually some people who dedicate their lives to a courageous and mystical pursuit of honor, valor and peace. The movies keep alive the rumor that there is a Force that is with you, and that this supernatural force of nature is not only real, but really believed in by millions of ordinary people.

Obi Wan Kenobi's "Force" is the same power of which the poets sing, from Shelley to Hopkins to Wordsworth to Dylan Thomas. It is the "Spirit of Beauty," the "force that through the green fuse drives the flower." It is the "dearest freshness deep down things," "unknown modes of Being," and the "awful shadow of some unseen Power." It is "a motion and a spirit, that impels all thinking things, all objects of thought and rolls through all things." For the Greek philosophers, this force of creation was called *Logos*, or the Word. *Logos* is the creative force of a God who speaks all things into being. The philosopher Heraclitus thought this essential life force was best symbolized by fire. In fact, when asked what essence the world was made of, Heraclitus—who lived six centuries before the Christians—foreshadowed their doxology with the words, "This world...was ever, is now, and ever shall be an everlasting Fire."

The fact that a Greek philosopher six centuries before Christ saw fire as the essential force tickles my imagination. Christianity is sometimes put down because it seems to have borrowed beliefs and ideas from other religions. So, for example, the critics see that Heraclitus thought the driving force of nature was fire, then they see that the Christian Holy Spirit is symbolized by fire and blame the Christians for stealing a good idea. But good ideas don't occur to just one person. Perhaps many people in many

154

different cultures have the same good idea simply because that idea is intrinsically true. Similarity does not prove influence. Or perhaps all the pre-Christian religious symbols of fire were hints and guesses—pointers to a real, world-fueling fire that Christians would someday call the Holy Spirit.

After all, the eternal flame burns in temples of every religion, and the fire burns throughout the ancient Hebrew stories in many forms. An angel with a fiery sword expels Adam and Eve from Eden. A fire burns on the altar as Abraham almost sacrifices his son. God speaks to Moses from a bush that burns, but is not consumed. The Jews are led from Egypt by a fiery pillar and establish a temple where lamps and altar fires burn perpetually to mark the presence of their God. Then the fire comes into specific focus on the Feast of Pentecost when, with a mighty wind, tongues of fire descend to enflame every Christian heart and mind.

That the force of nature is represented by fire is easy enough to understand. Indeed, fire is an excellent symbol for the life force because it is the most vivid and primeval energy source known to man. One can explore a symbol's origins, but what interests me are its implications. Heraclitus chose fire because he was trying to answer the question of how nature could be both one and many at the same time. In other words, how can there be an essential unity when there are so many individual entities? Heraclitus concluded that there had to an eternal essence that was itself unified and unchanging, but which enabled individual changing things to exist. Fire provided the perfect symbol for the philosopher because fire is constantly the same, yet constantly changing.

The most potent aspects of fire as an image are its usefulness and unity. It is an energy source that links everything. This is consistent with Heraclitus' philosophy, but it also sounds as modern as yesterday's physics and the new religion of the Jedi knights. Here is a force that binds together and dwells in all other things, and yet exceeds them. Here is a power that guides, directs and empowers transformation, a power that sponsors growth, inspires ideas and sparks change in the world. It is itself orderly, and therefore its direction is constantly toward unity, harmony and reconciliation of all that is broken, chaotic and fragmented. Furthermore, this "awful shadow of an unseen power" is not just a spectral, unseen force outside ourselves, is it? In a curious scene in the first *Star Wars* film, a Jedi knight explains to his apprentice that the force actually resides in every cell of his body. This makes sense, because if this force fires all things, then it must be in all things as well as outside all things. It must be both exterior and interior. In other words, it is not only "out there" but also "in here."

Up to this point there is very little with which most religious people could disagree. Buddhists, New Age Pagans, Christians, Jews and people who simply love a mountaintop and a good sunset may all agree on the existence of this benign force that works throughout nature and guides all human souls. But Christians have put a little bomb in this cozy agreement about the force of nature. The followers of Christ say that this same "force which through the green fuse drives the flower" finds a particular form in Jesus Christ. They insist that Jesus Christ is one with the force that created the world and keeps it going. The first Christian theologians put it quite neatly. Saint John picked up the Greek philosophical term *Logos* (the creative power of the universe) and said that the *Logos* became flesh and dwelt among human beings and that it was "full of grace and truth". Saint Paul said, "all things were created by Christ, and in him all things live and move and have their Being." This is where all the other people who are happy to believe in a "Life Force" get off the bus. It is, after all, a bit much to suggest that a backwoods preacher two thousand years ago was somehow also an incarnation of the cosmic force of nature—the very fiery energy source by which all things are created and sustained in life.

But what if we stand this on its head and push the question further? If this life force is a single force, then it is unified, and if it is unified, then it is simple. It is One. It is integrated with itself and with all physical things. If this is true, then this power must be a force for unity and harmony, not chaos and fragmentation. Therefore, if it is one and if it is a force for unity, then doesn't it demand expression in a single unified and integrated being?

What I mean is this: every aspect of life which is multiform and various, but which also claims some sort of unifying bond, requires that unity to be focused. A football team demands a coach, an orchestra demands a conductor, a country demands a head of state, a class demands a teacher, a church demands a priest, and a school demands a principal. Even when the group's unity is expressed through a committee that committee demands a chairman. Even when the group's voice is expressed in a vote that vote intends one person to win, and that one person is the focus of unity for all. For unity to be real it has to have a single voice, and a single voice can only be expressed through a single person.

You might say that it is sufficient that this unifying being remains a Holy Spirit, but part of its unifying action is to draw together the material and the physical realms, which are at war with one another. So if it is a unifying force between the material and spiritual realms, then the single unified and integrated being will need to be a physical being as well as a spiritual being.

To do this it has to focus down into a single being who unites the Spirit realm with the material realm. When you consider it that way, doesn't it seem not only credible, but necessary that at one place and at one time in history that unifying force of all nature should take a single human face, and speak through a single human voice? If it did, then that one human person would be a focus of unity, a head of state, a teacher, a priest and a head master not only for the whole human race, but for the whole of nature. This is precisely the claim Christians make for the God-Man Jesus Christ.

Furthermore, this voice of unity—this personification of the force of nature works to reconcile and draw all things to himself so that a fragmented, broken and chaotic created order might share increasingly in his unity, harmony and perfection. He does this by radiating his power out into the world like a magnet. The life force goes out from him and draws all people and all things back into a harmonious and ordered relationship with himself. This is what he meant when he breathed a new spirit on to his followers, and promised that a "comforter" would come who would teach them all things and draw them into a new kind of unity with him.

This centripetal force is what Christians call the "work of the Holy Spirit." The end result of this activity is to bring individuals into unity with Christ. But we speak here not of the unity binding football players, fellow citizens, or members of an orchestra. There is far more to it than that. What Christ means by being united with him is that we are actually drawn into a union with him that the New Testament likens to marriage. Even though they remain two distinct individuals, the spouses become one flesh. They permeate and interpenetrate one another, and when they unite physically they are sealing a union that is also mental and spiritual.

Stand on your head and take a fresh look at the implications of this. We are not talking about a religion that

159

simply puts people in touch with a benevolent force that will help them get through life. Or one that molds people to be good or to make the world a better place. We are not even offering a spirit guide that forms people to be as much like Jesus Christ as possible. Instead we are offering a fundamental and total overhaul. This is not just about saying prayers and being good. This is about being re-made into radiant beings who exist in a dynamic union with God. The New Testament says that by the action of the Spirit we have become God's sons and daughters. Christ was God's son, so in other words, by the work of the Holy Spirit we are being transformed into little Christs, and that is precisely what the word Christian originally meant. So this is not a religion that makes people good, but a religion that makes people gods. The first Christian theologians recognised this and called the process "divinization." They actually said, "In Christ God became man so that men could become gods."

Now if this is what Christianity is really about, then what a shallow farce we have made of it all when we reduce the whole thing to a system of doctrines, and rules of respectable behaviour. No wonder no one wants to be a Christian if the whole thing is no more than a set of table manners for social climbers! No wonder people run a mile when this stupendous potential of divinization is reduced to a list of regulations, seventeen hail Marys and a glory be. Similarly, if the work of the Holy Spirit is divinization, how puerile to reduce the whole matter, to a flurry of religious emotion featuring gooey music, "prosperity" miracles, waving hands, and waggling bottoms. If the whole business is about becoming everlasting beings of stupendous power and radiant goodness, then how ridiculous to turn the church into a social club, a political pressure group, an intellectual theology discussion group or a nauseating gaggle of pious do-gooders.

If the whole business is about divinization, then our work is cut out for us. The Force is with us, but we must also be with the Force, and this is no easy thing because every sinew of our being is twisted against such a goal, and needs to be untangled. The Holy Spirit is there to help, but we must first come alive to the fire that surges through all creation, and which surges in our own hearts. The power to be transformed is real, and it becomes real to individuals through a mysterious and frightening mechanism. And that mechanism is called death.

Death to the old ego, the twisted personality, is the first step in the transformation. This is why you cannot live unless you die, and this is why the Christian continually turns to the death and resurrection of Jesus Christ—because through that action, a transaction takes place. Through his death and rising again, Christ embraces the forces of chaos and destruction that lead to death. In rising again, he defeats those powers and releases a new force that draws all things back into unity and peace. From that crunch point he gives us the power to become the sons of God. In other words, he enables us to be remade in his image. There at his resurrection, the force that created the world burst forth with a new fire. There the fire that will draw all things into a final reconciliation was unleashed like a crash of lightning which flashes across the sky. In that moment the whole of life was turned upside down and became unexpectedly and terrifyingly new. There at the resurrection the life force bolted out to grab me, take me into itself, and change me into all that I was created to be. Through that death and resurrection the Holy Spirit made perfect in him is made perfect in me. There a new kind of life is possible, because there, as Gerard Manley Hopkins put it, "in a flash, in a trumpet crash, I am all at once what Christ is, since he was what I am," and there, "this Jack, joke, poor potsherd, patch, matchwood, immortal diamond, is immortal diamond."

CHAPTER FIFTEEN

The Universal Corner Shop

...The holy Catholic Church...

I T IS FAR EASIER to imagine that all religions are human inventions than that they are divine institutions, but what is easy is rarely good or true. It seems that religion—especially religious institutions—are human inventions. After all, why should God in heaven be concerned about such things as who is ordained as a priest or what makes a sacrament valid or whether the pope should have temporal power or how the presbytery should appoint a pastor or whether the parish council should be elected or appointed? Surely God has better things to do than be concerned with committees and councils and synods and standing orders.

This is where the Catholic Church once again stands the ordinary man-from-Missouri "common sense" assumptions on their head, for the Catholic Church claims to be both human and divine, and as such she claims to be not only a reflection of Christ himself, but a kind of incarnation of Christ himself.

Therefore we are confronted with what seems to be a lumbering, antique institution of byzantine complexity and frustrating bureaucracy; here is an archaic collection of buildings and books and rules and regulations and rubrics, dispensations and doctrines and dogmas, all of which seem to be made up by ordinary people to solve ordinary problems. And yet, within this seemingly top-heavy human organization, there lives a spirit of something else—something extraordinarily supernatural and eternal.

Trying to discern the divine within the details is one of the contradictory delights of being a Catholic—that somehow within all the very frail and often vile humanity within the universal Church, there is also a filament of light and life. The Catholic Church, like some of her members, appears to be a corrupt politician or a corpulent potentate or a ragged beggar or a deranged old woman, and then you discover that the politician is a saintly statesman, the potentate is an unexpectedly blessed pope; the ragged beggar is St. Francis and the mad old homeless woman is Mother Teresa.

One of the delightful things about converting to the Catholic Church is that it is still shocking. If you want to be a nonconformist, upset people's expectations and be genuinely subversive, become a Catholic. One of the most engaging things about the holy Catholic Church is what people think when they hear the phrase "Holy Catholic Church." Mention the name of almost any other religion and you will probably evoke a yawn. Mention "Holy Catholic Church" and you are bound to get a strong response, and most often that response is negative. Since Jesus Christ said, "Woe unto you, when all men shall speak well of you," it would seem that the Catholic Church is particularly blessed in this regard.

One of the most powerful hints that her claims are authentic is that the Catholic Church is barely tolerated and often attacked by nearly everyone who is outside it. That is exactly what Jesus told his followers to expect, so when a particular church is regularly vilified, persecuted and attacked it somehow makes it seem authentic. It is true that adversity makes strange bedfellows, and there is no bed more full of opposites than the anti-Catholic bed. So all sorts of Protestants, from snake handlers to suave theologians, are suddenly allies in their attacks on Rome. Antipathy towards the Catholic Church unites Communists and Ku Klux Klan members, Anglicans and Atheists, Methodists and Mormons. When faced with the ancient foe of the Roman Church, feminists embrace Freemasons and anarchists link arms with actual fascists.

Try a little experiment. Just for fun, tell people you have decided to become a Catholic. Your upscale friends will tease you for liking plastic snowstorm paperweights with miniature basilicas inside, paintings of Madonnas on black velvet, and pictures of Jesus with googly eyes. At the same time, your friends who pride themselves on being "plain folk" will blame you for a sudden interest in Baroque architecture, lacy vestments and Monteverdi masses. Educated colleagues will denounce you for joining an ignorant and unthinking religion that demands blind obedience, while your less learned friends will think you have been seduced by canon law, Jesuit casuistry and the subtleties of Thomism. Your democratic critic will blame you for being elitist, while the snob will smile sadly and say that you have chosen to mix with peasants, Mexican maids and Polish plumbers. "Spiritual" friends will be incredulous at your acceptance of a rigid, dogmatic and hierarchical system, while your theologically minded friends will say you have gone in for mysticism and mushy spirituality. Your liberal friends will shake their heads in dismay at the thought that you can submit to such a tyrannical, authoritarian and misogynist regime—while your conservative friends won't understand how you can possibly agree with a Church that promotes social welfare programs, discourages the death penalty, and is in favor of ecology, ecumenism and interfaith dialogue.

If such a great chorus of humanity could agree on exactly what they thought was wrong with the Church, then we might have to defer to them. But since the attacks are on totally contradictory fronts, don't we have to suspect that there might be a problem not with the attacked, but with the attackers? What is it about the Catholic Church that warrants such disapproval? Is there any other organization in the world that is so commonly misunderstood, mocked and maligned by various groups of people who cannot agree on anything else?

This is a genuine curiosity, but isn't there something in this paradox that rings true? Doesn't the fact that so many people are annoyed by the Catholic Church make it perversely attractive? Doesn't this weird contradiction make you want to join? After all, where else can you enjoy the delicious feeling of belonging to a subversive undercover army that is at the same time one of the most established and venerable of organizations? Where else can you belong to an elite group of initiated members while also affirming your membership in the whole family of the human race? Only here can you belong to a rag-tag company of sinners on earth while also being numbered amongst the whole company of heaven.

This contradiction demands an explanation. The reason the Catholic Church both agrees and disagrees with everybody is because she constantly tries to agree with somebody who is above and beyond everybody else. If I am sitting in London but have plans to climb Mount Everest, then as I set out on my adventure, I will agree with everyone who is travelling East, but I will also disagree with everyone who is stopping at Paris, Rome, Dubai or Delhi. This doesn't mean I am totally against everyone else who is travelling East. I may travel quite a long way with someone who is headed for the Himalayas, but eventually we will have to part company.

Truth is the Church's Mount Everest. For Catholics it rises majestically, a peak that's worth climbing "because it's *there*." The truth cannot be altered by circumstances of politics, fashions or trends. At the same time, climbing the mountain called truth is an arduous and risky business. There are many wrong turnings on the way and all too many chances to fall over an edge or plunge into a crevasse, and certainly members of the Catholic Church have stumbled and fallen many times in their ascent up the mountain.

Despite all her problems and human failures, the Catholic Church has developed an uncanny nose for truth. But the Catholic Church realizes that the worst enemy of the truth is not a lie, but a half-truth. Lies are easy to see through. Half-truths are cloudy and thick. Being opposed to such cloudiness, the Catholic Church has developed a knack for sniffing out where a particular position is right and where it is wrong. That is why, as soon as you take a strong position on almost anything, you will find that the Catholic Church agrees with you on the one hand and says you are wrong on the other. We all know how annoying a know-it-all is, so perhaps that is why so many people become so very annoyed by the Catholic Church.

But people seem to forget that the Catholic Church has been around for a rather long time. Here is an organization that has continued to thrive for the last two thousand years, and is still going strong. Is there another religious, political or social organization still chugging on since the days of Imperial Rome? My point is that the Catholic Church has seen quite a few trends come and go. She has two thousand years worth of human history and experience to reflect on, and she realizes that most of our mistakes have been made before. Can she be blamed if, like a wise old woman, she draws on her vast experience to help her children succeed in life? If she nags a bit too much, shakes a bony finger and "tut-tuts," well, maybe she can't help it.

People are often annoyed by the claims of the Holy Catholic Church at an intellectual level, but more often the reaction is an emotional one. When people hear the words, "Holy Catholic Church," they may imagine nightmarish scenes from the Spanish Inquisition, the imposing façade of St Peter's in Rome, and a labyrinthine power structure with innumerable sinister men dressed in red and black. Perhaps they have pictures of grim-faced nuns in starchy costume thrashing schoolchildren into submission. I am not denying that all this may be a part of Catholicism, but it is a part of the whole faith, just as a chamber of horrors is part of the amusement park. We would be wrong to assume that the spooks in the ghost house are the whole story. Even so, these lurid impressions of the "Holy Catholic Church" are mostly emotional reactions to what is essentially a lucid and precise term.

To cut through the lurid to find the lucid, it is worth looking at the words more simply. The first word of this phrase is "holy". At once we are struck by a word with vivid connotations. All our own images of "holiness" come flooding in. For most people, "holiness" is the same as piety, and being pious is associated with wide-eyed missionaries or eager boys with their trousers hitched up, sporting big smiles and bigger Bibles. Perhaps when we hear "holy" we think of an endless round of dreary religious services, frightening moral exhortations and the doom and gloom of large dark houses. Holiness, in other words, is associated with all that is dull about religion.

But in this phrase of the creed the word "holy" has a purer and simpler meaning. It means "whole" or complete." It means simple, total, integrated and unified. This meaning of "holy" is linked with goodness in a different way. If "holy" means "whole" or "integrated" or "complete," then a thing that is "holy" is good not because it is moral, and not because it is trying hard to be better than everything else, but because it is simply what it should be. And for a thing to be what it ought to be is for it to be natural, and when a thing is natural, it is good. So when we say that the Church is "holy," we are not saying that she is always totally clean and pure and pious and sinless. Instead, we are saying that she is whole and complete, unified and integrated. In other words, her teaching, her practice, her inspiration, history and example form an integrated and beautiful unity.

This doesn't mean the Holy Catholic Church is devoid of moral goodness. Indeed, the most radiant examples of human goodness are found amongst the saints. But the moral goodness is not what makes the Holy Catholic Church holy. What makes it holy is its wholeness. Now what really interests me about this wholeness is that for something to be whole and complete, it actually has to include some evil as well as some good. If something is real and solid, it reflects light and casts shadows. In other words, for a human institution to be whole and real it has to include the human struggle against evil in all its forms. That is why part of the "holiness" of the Catholic Church encompasses evil popes, heretic burners, and bishops' mistresses. What I mean by this outrageous statement is that the whores and heretics are part of the battle. The Church is whole because the whole of human experience is there, and isn't that just what you would expect to find in any family or institution that is real? This is not to condone either the burning of heretics or the burning of lust, it is simply to acknowledge that the battle is always present, and that this makes the story sound authentic. The history of the Catholic Church reads like the Old Testament. It is full of blood and thunder. It is full of real people who enter the great battle and sometimes win and sometimes lose. In fact, wouldn't you be suspicious if everything were totally spotless, squeaky clean and sinless? Wouldn't you smell a rat? That sort of squeaky-clean Church wouldn't be holy. It would be full of holes. It would leak and be ultimately incredible.

The second word in this phrase is "Catholic." I am not sure what people think of when they hear the word, but before I was a Catholic I immediately imagined large, dark churches where banks of candles gutter before austere images of dead saints. I imagined corpulent Renaissance popes sending armies out to fight while they told Michelangelo how to paint. I imagined altars and sacrifices, priests in black, prayers with beads, and people going up steps on their knees. I imagined hordes of Spanish people dressed in hoods carrying torches, and towering platforms with tottering Virgins. There may be a whole range of other impressions which the word "Catholic" summons up, and they may be bright or shadowy images depending on our own experience. But to cut through all those personal images, the word "Catholic" simply means "universal." In other words, it exists and thrives everywhere and at every time, and has done so since it was founded by Jesus Christ two thousand years ago.

This is another astounding fact about the Catholic Church that is easily overlooked. In an age of multinational companies, the Catholic Church is really the only multinational religion. It is global. The other religions, sects and cults are confined by all sorts of boundaries. Sometimes they are limited by the theology or politics of their founders and the circumstances in which they lived. So the Protestant Christians are defined and limited by the theological and political events of the sixteenth century. The Anglicans and Eastern Orthodox groups are defined and limited by their national and ethnic culture and history. You may find an African Anglican, but he is far more English than an African Catholic is Italian. The other world religions have tried to migrate, but they do not travel well. It is difficult to be both an Englishman and a Muslim, and I have never known an all-American Hindu. Catholicism, on the other hand, has an amazing capacity to adapt and survive. Like a weed, it can grow anywhere, and when you pull it out it keeps coming back.

I am not saying that the other Christian groups or the other religions are all wrong. Catholics recognize the truth and goodness in all other religions apart from devil worship (and even that may have some good in it since it encourages people to believe in hell). The fact that the Catholic Church affirms the goodness found in other religions is another sign of her magnificent universality. "If there is truth there," she seems to say, "we will have it. We recognize it. We can make room for it."

No other religion, sect or cult dares to make such universal claims as the Catholic Church. But while the Catholic Church claims to be universal, it is also as local as the corner shop. If you want to find the Catholic Church, do not go to Rome. That is simply where the international offices are located. The real Catholic Church is St. Walburga's or St. Mary Magdalene's around the corner from your house. There the whole universal Catholic Church, majestic and monumental down the ages, is present in a local microcosm. There you will find Catholics from every social class, every race and every age group. Other Christian groups gather according to social, economic and educational divisions. In the Catholic Church rich and poor, young and old, black and white, professional and unemployed, men and women, liberal and conservative, saints and sinners all gather together in a unity that is, quite simply, astounding. In what human grouping of any kind will you find such a vast array of different individuals united around a shared goal?

This universal corner shop is what we mean by "Church." Again, the word carries a vast range of personal meanings. When you hear the word "church," you may think of any kind of building from a white clapboard Baptist Church on a hill in South Carolina to the cathedral of Notre Dame. "Church" may make you think of musty hymn books, kneelers, boring sermons and droning organs. When you hear "church," you may think of pretty places to get married or somber rooms for funerals. But the word "church" simply means convocation or gathering together, and it is this vastly varied gathering together of humanity that we celebrate in the Holy Catholic Church.

Down through the ages, people have had dreams of one united human family. From the Tower of Babel to the United Nations, men have been trying to establish a single world system. Whether it is with armies or politics or economics, the underlying goal of human endeavor has been to knit together a pan-global, unifying system for all humanity. The dream is that divisions will cease and mankind can live together in harmony, unity and brotherly love. But all the emperors and economists have missed the point. All the generals and general secretaries, all the presidents and prime ministers have not picked up on the fact that this universal convocation of humanity already exists, and has for two thousand years. It has an integrated work force. It has over a billion loyal members of the human race. It has a centralized leadership that shapes the minds and the hearts of its members. It binds together the whole human race with shared dreams, shared aspirations, and a common goal for nothing less than the salvation of the world and the reconciliation and unification of all human beings. That organization is the Holy Catholic Church, and while all the other empires rise and fall, she quietly carries on her mission. Despite persecution from without and corruption from within, in every age she carries on her mission, confident in the promise of her founder that even the gates of hell cannot prevail against her.

CHAPTER SIXTEEN

Encyclopaedic Sanctity

...The communion of saints...

ONE OF THE assumptions of the modern world is that each individual must know himself and express himself and be himself and have high self-esteem. But the irony of it is that I cannot know myself except in relationship with other people. It is only as I live and love or quarrel or play or fight with other people that I actually discover who I am.

This is because man is a social being. It is not good for man to be alone, so from the beginning, God created a companion. And as soon as there is one other person, we start to be in communication, in commerce, in communion with that other person and then every other person. If this is so, then individualism starts to seem like a strange aberration, a weird perversion of what it means to be human.

Catholicism insists that religion, like all life, is a family affair. You can't be a solitary Catholic. Even hermits who live in caves on mountains in Greece are part of a community of other hermits. Even the Carthusians—the strictest of monks, who live in prison-like cells and observe strict silence—live within a community and meet once a week to chat and laugh and quarrel and discuss their lives.

From the family life of the Hebrew people to the gathering of twelve men around a supper table, the Catholic faith has been anti-individualist. This is not because the individual is devalued, but because he can only flourish within a family and a community.

So to be a Christian is to be in common—to be in communion with others who are also striving to walk the pilgrim path, and to be in this community is a way for each individual to open up and out, to become far more than they ever could have been on the power of individualism alone. This may sound trite or yawn-inducingly mundane, but those who have truly lived within community in an intimate way tell us that personal transactions take place at a profound level, and the person who dwells in one finds not oblivion but fulfillment.

Anyone who has visited a Catholic cathedral in Spain will have to admit that the experience is a surreal cross between a religious shrine, a wax-museum chamber of horrors, and a medieval market. First of all, the place is likely to be noisy, with lots of chattering people doing everything from praying to sightseeing to selling postcards. The noise of clucking poultry may make you wonder if you've stumbled into the livestock pen, but then when you have a look, you may well see a cage of chickens suspended from the ceiling. Wander further and you will see a painting of a levitating saint in ecstasy or a bank of candles guttering in front of a Madonna dressed in cloth of gold with a little crown on her head. There will be flowers, old ladies dressed in black wearing veils, little boys playing hide-and-seek, and a line of people standing by something that looks like an ornate privy but which you know to be a confessional. If you turn the corner into a side chapel you may find the arm bone of a saint or a life-sized crucifix complete with every detail of Jesus Christ's suffering. There is a famous such cross in Burgos that actually has human hair, glass eyes, and was reputed to be covered with human skin (it turned out to be cowhide.)

All of this is horrific to those who like their religion (like their lives) kept sensible, clean and neat. It is also distasteful for those who prefer to keep their religion lofty, sublime and intellectual. Spanish Christianity, complete with chickens and cow-hide crucifixes, is a reminder that in the creed we say that we believe in the "communion of saints." Normally when people say this phrase, they are saying that they are in the same club as all the Christians who have ever been alive in every place and at every time. This is fine, but it was pointed out to me some time ago that the word "the saints" actually used to mean "the holy things." In other words, when you say "I believe in the communion of saints," you are saying that you are united not only with the holy people, but with everything everywhere that is good, beautiful, true and holy.

One of the curious things about the Catholic expression of Christianity is that this communion with everything that is true, beautiful and holy is a *reality*. Everything which is true, whether it is an attractive truth or a terrible one, no matter what religion, sect or cult it comes from, finds a place within the vast cathedral that is the Church. Take any tradition or belief at all from any religion, and if it is beautiful and true, or even if it is just fun or fascinating or useful, it can be found within Catholicism. Let me give a few examples from the major religions. The strength of Islam is its passionate devotion to One God and to the teachings of the Book. In their case the book is the Koran. Catholicism also affirms with passion the greatness of the one God and the truth of the Book (in their case, the Bible). Buddhism encourages a sublime transcendent spirituality, with monks and celibacy and a life of contemplation. Likewise Catholicism. Judaism lives out a dynamic roller-coaster history of religion in which the people of God have tried to follow the law of God. Same with Catholics. Hindus enjoy a religion replete with statues, candles, ornate temples, colorful festivals and terrible myths. Catholics do too. Do New Agers love chants, adore nature, and employ incense and meditation? So do Catholics. Do Shintoists venerate their ancestors? Catholics offer masses for theirs.

The same applies to all of the various Christian sects. Do Anglicans have sublime literature, music and architecture? Catholics revel in these things. Do Pentecostals speak in tongues and sing happy choruses? Plenty of Catholics do too. Do the narrow-minded Brethren say that only members of their church may come to communion? The Catholics also preserve their holiest things for initiates. Do Evangelical Christians love the Bible? The New Testament was compiled and edited by Catholics, who are still among the world's best scripture scholars. Do the Amish eschew modern materialism to live a simple, austere and holy life? So do Catholic monks and nuns. These are but a few examples. They can be replicated time and time again, so that it is most true that when Catholic Christians say "I believe in the communion of the saints" they are also saying, "I am in a union with all holy things."

The reason for this is that, beneath all the negative propaganda and the sour impressions of bad Catholics, the Catholic Church is essentially a church that says "yes." We say that if a thing is good and beautiful and holy, then it must be true, and if it is true, we will find a place for it. This is because a person is most often right in what he affirms and wrong in what he denies. When do most people begin to fall out with the Catholic Church? When they begin to deny something which Catholics hold dear. So if you come into the Spanish Cathedral and splutter, "But what are those chickens doing here! They're making a huge mess all over the floor!" you are denying something that is actually quite fun and unexpected. The good Catholic will tell you to stop being such a spoilsport. They are likely to say, "Those chickens were here before you were. Let them be." So it is whenever a critic tries to destroy something beautiful, good, true, or just plain fun within Catholicism. Do they come in and say, "You can't believe in a medieval superstition like transubstantiation!" "You can't possibly have an all-powerful pope in this age of democracy!" And Catholics reply, "Oh, do leave it alone! It was here before you came along. If you don't understand it, that's your fault, but destroying what you don't understand is the way of the boor and the vandal."

So Catholic Christianity embraces everything good, and that really summarizes what a saintly person is as well. The most famous saint of the modern age was a teenaged French girl called Thérèse Martin, who said, "I will have all!" She wasn't being greedy, she was simply accepting everything in the universe as a good gift from God. For her that included an excruciating death at an early age, but this too she accepted as a gift.

When an ordinary person gets to the stage where even pain is understood as a special gift from heaven, then that ordinary person is either mad or they have been transformed into something greater than an ordinary person. The first Christians thought this was possible. They really did believe that Jesus Christ came not only to rescue the human race, but to transform it into his likeness. This means that individual human beings could actually become like Christ. The ramifications of this belief are astounding, for if Jesus Christ was God in the flesh, then these ordinary mortals came to realize that the long-term effect of becoming like Jesus Christ was to become gods themselves.

This is the other meaning of the phrase "communion of saints." It means that in this life we can be in constant contact with real human beings who have experienced this transformation. Furthermore, when we say we believe in the communion of saints, we believe the saints in heaven can actually do good on earth. On her terrible deathbed Thérèse Martin had the audacity to claim, "I will spend my heaven doing good on earth."

Suddenly an amazing realization dawns—that to become a saint is to become a little god or goddess. There is an old legend that God created human beings to repopulate heaven after all the rebellious angels got in a huff and left to follow Satan. The process of this mass emigration from earth to heaven entails becoming saints, and being divinized—transformed into the likeness of Christ, the god-man. Furthermore, if some people have become saints, if some people have been divinized, then it is possible for more, even all, people to be transformed in this way. This is the astounding potential that is on offer to every person who professes the Christian faith. The death of Jesus Christ does not simply cover over our imperfections. It gives us the power to change our worst faults into our greatest strengths.

Saying we believe in "the communion of saints" means we are in the company of people who have been divinized, and if we are in their company, then we are one of them, and if we are one of them, then we are called to be like them and do what they have done. If this is true, then suddenly the whole Christian faith becomes a lifelong arduous journey of growth and change. If this is true, then the spiritual life is not just a matter of wandering up a gentle hill to enjoy the view. It is more like the ascent up a mountain which dwarfs earthly Everest. The way is steep and the weather sharp. The spiritual ascent is more like scaling a sheer cliff face than a stroll up a hill. We are all called to put on our boots and train for the ascent. We are summoned to grapple with the ropes and pitons, negotiate the ledges, gasp in the thin air. And then we face the precipice, the narrow crumbling ledge, and the yawning abyss.

If you are in that company, your whole life revolves around the ascent of that mountain. You come to realize that this is what you are here for. This is the whole point of life—indeed, of the universe. You are here to be divinized, to be transformed into all that you were created to be. So you either decide to live in communion with saints, or not. You either climb the mountain, or don't. Even if it takes your whole life and many years of struggle in the life to come, climb the mountain you must. There is no room here for half measures. So that same teenaged girl who allowed this awesome and radiant transformation to take place in her life says to us, "You cannot be half a saint, you must be a whole saint or no saint at all!"

We may be offered an awesome glory, but we are also called to an awesome task. We are right to be daunted. But the ascent is the way to claim all things holy and infinitely precious for our own. Why are we surprised if they are costly? Did we think that all things eternal in heaven and earth would be ours for a bargain-basement price? While the reality of this truth may cause alarm, there is also cause for comfort because in the ascent, we are not alone. We climb with an army of family and friends. And at every moment, those who have gone before are just beyond us on the next ridge, calling down, "We will give you a hand up! Do not be afraid! Come further up and further in!"

CHAPTER SEVENTEEN

The Metanoia Mentality

...The forgiveness of sins...

THAT IRASCIBLE AND revolutionary poet e.e.cummings has a line, "even on a sunday may I be wrong, for whenever men are right they are not young." There is something innocent and free and youthful in admitting you are wrong, and something pompous and unpleasant and ancient in admitting you are right. Being "wrong" is being foolish and carefree, and shrugging with a grin at the human comedy and tragedy. Being "right" is uptight and self-righteous and grim-lipped in the face of human frailty and failure. At the heart of faith, therefore, is this delightful insistence on standing the human instinct to be right all the time on its head and insisting instead on being wrong.

When we insist at least on the possibility that we may not always be right, and this becomes a foundational outlook on ourselves and others, then the whole world is turned upside down. If we are not right, then most anything could happen. If we are uncertain, then nothing is certain and we are open to the new possibilities and perspectives that our "being right" would never have allowed.

This disturbing new way of thinking lies at the heart of the strange Christian insistence on this experience called "repentance." For "repentance" is simply a theological way of saying, "I'm wrong," and confession is the active and liturgical way of doing the same. Once the foundational assumption that "I'm right" is replaced with the foundational assumption that "I'm wrong," the human being is young again and can learn again and can be curious again and can at last begin to grow again. Of course, the only way the individual can have the freedom and *joie de vivre* of being wrong is in the confidence that someone else is right. In other words, we confess with a joyful spirit, "I am wrong, but God will put it right."

Isn't it curious how confession is acceptable—fashionable even—within the realm of self-help and group therapy, while it is considered dark, neurotic and "guilt-ridden" in the realm of religion? If you go to a therapist you will be encouraged to spill the beans, because it is healthy. If you receive counseling, you will be expected to haul all the skeletons out of all the cupboards without shame. In an Alcoholics Anonymous group, the person next to you will be encouraged to say, "I'm George, and I'm an alcoholic." But if you go to church and the person next to you shakes

186

your hand and says, "I'm Mildred, and I'm a sinner," you will have your fears confirmed that the church is full of fruitcakes.

But Mildred shouldn't be blamed for being honest, any more than George should. Surely one of the most obvious things any human being can say about themselves is, "I'm a sinner." Being a sinner simply means that we haven't reached the unbelievably glorious potential for which we were created. As the New Testament puts it, "For all have sinned, and come short of the glory of God." If we are created in God's image and are destined for divinization, then to have fallen short of God's glory means we have missed the target. This fact ought to be an almost constant, nagging realization within our lives. Our first waking moment when we decide to stay in bed for an extra twenty minutes is our first little realization that we're doing less than our best. If we were operating to our potential, we would have sprung out of bed much earlier and got on with the creative, abundant and exciting life that could be ours. And yet it is our instinct to justify our laziness, and that too confirms the point that there is a kink in our nature.

But saying there is a kink in our nature is not the same as saying that we are all evil through and through. Simple observation tells me that I am not all bad, and neither are most people. In fact, even the bad things we do are often only mistakes or misunderstandings. The idea that we are totally evil through and through is one of those theological pathologies that have damaged millions of lives. The fact remains that we are created in God's image, so it is impossible for us to be totally and utterly evil. Instead, the image of God has been wounded or marred by our sinful inclinations. We need to be healed. The kink needs to be straightened out. The complex knot of our motives, desires, decisions and actions needs to be untangled.

So to say, "I am a sinner," is not to grovel in the dust, reveling in self-loathing. It is simply being honest about ourselves and admitting that while we've got strengths, we've also got weaknesses. While we've learned a lot, we've still got a lot to learn. Saying, "I'm a sinner," is simply saying that "I'm not all that I could be." This is a negative definition of sin, but it is a good place to start. Very often, that missed potential becomes more than an absence of all that we could be, and becomes a positive *presence* of all that we shouldn't be. When my laziness at six-thirty turns into irritability at being disturbed, and I then yell at the kids, my lack of potential becomes not just something good undone, but something nasty done. To understand how very nasty we can be, we only have to examine what we do in private.

Furthermore, to comprehend how ultimately nasty human beings can be, we only have to turn to the annals of crime and the horrors of history. Hitler's holocaust, the bombing of the World Trade Center, the purges of Stalin, and the killing fields of Cambodia and Rwanda illustrate the monstrosity of man. The stories of the serial killers, the rapists and the child murderers remind each one of us of the truly demonic potential of human beings. Human beings are created to be divinized, but the sins of mankind remind us that the other option is to be demonized. The logic follows that if it is possible to become radiant eternal beings of goodness and light, then it is also possible to become gibbering monsters of unspeakable evil and darkness. So while the saints remind us that we can be divine, the monsters of the human race remind us that we can also be devilish. We must choose which path we will take. Will we scale the heights of divinization or slide into the abyss of demonization? When you think about it, there really isn't any other option. In the afterlife the chips are called in, the report card is given, and the winners and losers are announced. The final destiny is to burn either with the radiance of glory or the dark fires of damnation. There is no room on that side for mediocrity. Every journey ends up somewhere. It is better to decide on your destination while you are still on the journey, than to discover in the end that you have caught the wrong bus.

Say it: "I am a sinner." It is simply the first and most brutally honest admission that you have seen the way things are and that you want to make the right choice. Our natural instinct, however, is to say that we are not sinners. Our first inclination is to defend ourselves, blame the other person and justify what we have done. To really say, "I am a sinner," at the level of total reality requires a major shift in perception. There is a word for this fundamental shift of awareness. It is *metanoia* which means "turning around." In other words, to say, "I'm a sinner," requires a fundamental about-face. When Christians go on to say they believe in the "forgiveness of sins," they are saying that once we make the first admission that we are a sinner, and that we need something, that there is help available. There is a remedy for the sickness of sin. The knot can be untangled and the twist can be put straight.

In this connection, Christians (and Catholic Christians especially) are often blamed for spreading guilt. "Oh, the nuns at our school were forever making us feel guilty!" is the lament of the convent girl. But the nuns were there to teach children the truth, and it is an obvious truth that people *are* actually guilty. The method of imparting this truth may not always have been kind or loving, but the truth still remains. Guilt is a kind of pain that naturally accompanies sin. It is a built-in reminder that sin is a sickness, and that any sickness that remains untreated may very well turn nasty and cause an awful lot of pain, heartache and violence.

If you like, guilt is to sin what pain is to cancer. If you have cancer, you will eventually have pain. Likewise, if you are a sinner, eventually you will suffer from guilt. A good doctor doesn't say to you, "Oh my dear! Are you suffering pain? I will give you a pain killer and then you will feel better." On the contrary, the good doctor gathers his courage and says, "Let's talk straight. You are feeling pain because you have cancer, and the only remedy is going to be surgery, followed by an awful dose of chemotherapy, and even then, you may not pull through."

In a similar way, a good priest or nun does not say, "Are you feeling guilty darling? Never mind, you are not really a sinner. You are just suffering low self-esteem. When you feel bad about yourself, it is just a result of your sad home life. Just tell yourself you are a nice person and you will feel better." No, a good priest or nun says, "What are you feeling guilty about? Have you sinned? The remedy is to confess the sin, accept forgiveness, then go and make amends." This process seems to me to be utter common sense. Any child who has fought on the playground knows that if he has done something wrong, he needs to say "sorry," and then put things right. It is the same with any person's fault. Although the circumstances may be far more complicated, the principle is the same.

The only thing that remains is the concept of forgiveness, and forgiveness is one of those quirky ideas that Jesus Christ brought into the world. We take it for granted that saying "sorry" and forgiving people is the way to go. But it is not so in other cultures. In fact, there are whole rafts of other ways for people to deal with things that have gone wrong. People might sacrifice virgins to appease the gods. They might pay a ransom to an injured party to put things right. They might cut themselves with knives, starve themselves, or dance like a whirling dervish to satisfy angry gods. The most common recourse instead of forgiveness is revenge. And revenge makes sense. An eye for an eye and a tooth for a tooth seems to be a rather logical way of dealing with the problem.

But Jesus Christ comes in with this absurd idea of forgiveness. Where does this idea come from? Have you thought what this really means? It means that someone has the final power to either hold our sin against us or to lift the charge. Why should anyone have the nerve to claim such power? Where does it come from? This is precisely the question the religious leaders asked of Christ himself. When he forgave people they said, "Who does this man think he is? Only God can forgive sins." They were right, of course. Only God can forgive sins because only God can be the judge, and only God can be the judge because only God knows everything. Therefore, only God can forgive sins and mete out just punishment. So when he claimed to forgive sins, Jesus Christ was making a huge metaphysical claim. He was claiming that he himself had been given the authority on earth to do just that.

This is the crunch point of the Christian faith—that Christianity is not first and foremost a set of theologically good ideas. It is not a system of decent morality. It is not first and foremost a religion of proper ritual and the right philosophy. It is a faith of forgiveness. The simple transaction is this: Human beings say, like George at the Alcoholics Anonymous meeting, "I am a sinner." Jesus Christ then says, "I forgive you, and to prove that I have forgiven you, I will take the punishment for your sin myself, and if you accept this astounding sacrifice, then your slate will be wiped clean. You can get a fresh start, and then with your cooperation we can solve your sin problem once and for all. Furthermore, if you persevere, you will receive the power to become like me."

This transaction is not a once-and-done affair. It is done once, and then done over and over again. An old monk was asked what he did in the monastery all day. His reply was, "We fall and get up again. We fall and get up again." If the Christian life is scaling a monumental mountain, then at times we lose our step and fall down a crevasse. We get knocked off the ledge and grab a tiny lip of rock by our fingertips. Sometimes we stumble so badly that we plummet toward our deaths with only the thin but unbreakable line of forgiveness to save us from our fall. At times we climb the mountain in a driving snowstorm, unable to see the way. We may even clamber on hands and knees, but still we climb. In fact, on this particular mountain we may even come to realize that our best progress is made on our knees.

Because of this, you can immediately tell the authentic Christian from the phoney. The phoney one thinks he has climbed the mountain already. The authentic Christian doubts whether he has actually started yet. This is one of the tricks of the kingdom: the ones who are furthest along really do believe they are at the back, and the ones who think they are furthest up the mountain really haven't left the training camp yet. It is true that the last shall be first, and the first last.

That is why the Christian who is furthest along the journey repeats a constant prayer, which is simply, "Lord Jesus Christ, Son of God, have mercy on me, a sinner." He has developed a *metanoia* mentality. He is constantly turning around, constantly checking his instinct to be right and acknowledging that he is wrong. To one who does not understand, this constant prayer sounds like the depths of doom and gloom religion. Nothing could be further from the truth. Instead of being a paean of pessimism, it is a prayer of peace. Rather than being a muttering of despair, it is a word of utter joy. For in that prayer the simple soul repeats the essential human truth. In that prayer he affirms the fundamental condition of the human race, and declares with total dignity, clarity and joy what it means to be human: that I need help. I cannot climb alone. I am lost and need to be found.

CHAPTER EIGHTEEN

Cannibals, Crocodiles and Corpses

...The resurrection of the body...

I T WOULD ALL be so much easier if Christians believed that the soul after the physical death simply floated wispily up to some ethereal place in the sky to sort of hover about in a diaphanous gown in a place of light that is beautiful and vast and ectoplasmic, like those photographs we see from the Hubble space telescope. It would all be so much easier if we just became ghosts who swooped about like puffs of smoke.

Unfortunately, this is not the Christian view of life after death. Instead, we say in the creed that we believe in the "resurrection of the body," and if we actually stop and think (rather than parrot it mindlessly), it will hit us between the eyes with the force of a baseball bat. "What, shall this pudgy, balding body of mine be saved in some way? You mean, it's worth that much? I was hoping to trade it in for a newer model."

The radical proposals in the Christian creed really are upsetting, for we are expected to believe that these bodies that we see aging every day and that we know will one day rot and decay into dust are supposed to go on living, somewhere and somehow. But given the other tenets in the creed, there is no other option.

All the points of the creed intersect and interact, and the fact of the matter is that *there are facts in matter.* That is to say, matter has been penetrated by Truth. In the incarnation of Jesus Christ, the Eternal took fleshly form. That which was pure spirit became something physical and as a result the physical realm was changed forever. Something changed. The nature of reality changed. The physical is infused with a new dimension of life, and if this is true, then it reverberates across every galaxy of the cosmos and reverberates down into every cell of the physical creation and finally reaches the very question of what happens to me when I die—not just my soul, but my body as well.

Any school child who thinks about the resurrection of the body soon starts asking delightfully gruesome questions. After all, if they've ever seen a cat hit by a car, and then been to a funeral and seen Uncle Mitch in the casket and watched the coffin being lowered into the ground, they have a pretty good idea what happens. It doesn't take long to figure out that dead bodies decay and that Uncle

Mitch, who sat them on his knee for a story and gave them huge bowls of ice cream, now lies very still in a box going all gooey like the cat by the roadside. Therefore, the difficulty of believing in the resurrection of the body soon hits home. To put it bluntly, how can the body be resurrected if worms have eaten it and turned it back into topsoil? The questions continue. What about Aunty Hazel who loved doing crosswords and amateur dramatics? She was cremated and her ashes can be seen in an urn on Uncle Bert's mantelpiece. Will those ashes be magically put back together again into an all-singing, all-dancing, puzzle-solving Aunty Hazel? Or what about people who were blown to bits by a bomb or were eaten by sharks or crocodiles or lions and tigers and bears... Oh my!

We don't want to insult God's accounting practices. We know he keeps track of every hair on our head, and know when every sparrow falls, but is he really going to repossess every molecule of Grandpa and Aunty Hazel and the missionaries who were eaten by cannibals? Will he track them all down and summon them all up to be put back together again like some vast cosmic jigsaw puzzle?

The question is a good one and ought to interest everyone because we all have a morbid curiosity about the gruesome details. That's why we slow down at road accidents. There are really only three ways around it. First, faced with the poetic foolishness of such an idea, we may simply opt for the atheist's solution and say there is no such thing as life after death. This would put us in a minuscule minority when faced with the huge number of human beings who do believe in life after death, but nevertheless, the atheist position, although it takes great faith and courage to adhere to, is one solution.

The second option is that there is no such thing as the resurrection of the body, and instead we continue to exist in a merely spiritual state. But when you stop to imagine such a state, it is impossible to do so. At least, it is impossible to do so while still retaining any sense in which a particular person continues to exist as the same particular person. As soon as we start imagining Aunty Hazel existing on the other side, but without a body, she ceases to be Aunty Hazel and becomes an ectoplasm or an amoeba— just an amorphous something. We might try to imagine Aunty Hazel as just her personality or spirit, but as soon as we do, her smiling face appears, and we remember her belting out "There's no business like show business." In other words, Aunty Hazel can't exist as just personality or spirit, because Aunty Hazel was always more than just a personality. She was a person. So if we believe in life after death but not the resurrection of the body, then we can't say a particular person continues to exist as that particular person. That's why some religions say that in the afterlife we get rid of bodies altogether and are simply absorbed back into the cosmic Spirit.

The third option is that we continue to exist as the people we are here and now, and to do that we have to have bodies of some sort. We have to have bodies to be who we are, because from day one who we are has always included a body. Therefore, if we say we believe in life after death, then somehow or other, no matter how ridiculous it seems, we also have to believe in the *resurrection body*.

But maybe when we considered the problem of corpses that had turned to dust and ashes or been eaten by crocodiles and cannibals, we were taking the physical solidity of our bodies a bit too seriously. This is easy to do because we are used to thinking of our bodies as "this too too solid flesh." We imagine that this hairy, smelly, frustrating and funny body which we occupy right here and right now is the one we have always had, and that it is really quite a permanent fixture of the universe. But of course, it isn't. Not only will it turn to dust and ashes one day, but the body we have now isn't the same one we've always had. In fact, over the course of every seven years or so, most of the cells of our body are replaced—so in a very real sense, the body I have now is a completely different one than the one that used to wear bell bottoms (for instance). By looking at old photographs I can see that the body I have now has grown from that other one, but it is clearly different. In fact, the body I have today has changed a bit since yesterday. Therefore, what we see as a solid, proprietary body is in fact quite a flexible thing. We are all shape-shifters. Our bodies are far more fluid and temporary than we think, and we mustn't be mislead simply because the shape-shifting takes place over two presidential terms.

I make this point to introduce the idea that although my physical body of cells and molecules changes every seven years or so, there is, nevertheless, another "body" which doesn't change. There is a physical part that is always me, despite the changes. That photograph of me as a child does not picture the same body, but it does picture the same person. This brings us to the meaning of the word "body." In the Latin form of the creed, we do not profess belief in the *corporis resurrectionem*, but in *carnis resurrectionem*. In other words, we don't profess belief in the resurrection of the "body," but of the "flesh." The theological definition of the word "flesh" comes from the Hebrews, who blessed the whole human race with a wonderfully sophisticated religious idea. They rejected the obvious idea that our bodies are shells or vehicles for our souls. Instead, they thought that the flesh and the soul were permanently integrated and united. For them, "flesh" means much more than just the physical body. It means the whole person with all the gifts of body, mind and spirit fused into one physico-spiritual being.

If this is so, then rather than the soul living in the body as a person lives in a house, we should think of the soul dwelling in every cell of the body. Increasingly, the biologists understand the mind in this way. So the mind does not seem to be limited only to the brain, but it is spread by the nervous system throughout the whole body. The soul, then, does not exist in one part of the body, but infuses the entire body down to the tiniest cell and molecule. Evidence of this is in the weird things that sometimes happen with organ transplants. The recipients of new organs are known to inexplicably assume character traits and tastes which they never had before, but which their donor had when he was alive.

So if the mind dwells in every cell, then maybe the soul does too. This is easy enough to suggest as a theory, but let us stand it on its head and say that if the soul dwells in every cell of the body, then maybe a bit of the body dwells in every part of the soul as well. After all, if we are a totally fused, body-and-soul creation, then this would follow. We have all heard of the old soldier who still feels pain in his amputated leg even when it isn't there. Sometimes he even reaches to scratch empty air because his absent leg itches so much. That indicates that, just as the mind and soul inhabit the body, so the body (even when part of it has been cut off) inhabits the mind and the soul. If that is so, then there exists a kind of "soul body," which we could call the resurrection body. It has continuity with our mortal physical body (as my boyhood body has continuity with the present fat and bald one), and it is derived from that body. However, it is the soul version, and is not subject to decay and change.

This shouldn't be so hard to imagine, because, as I've already pointed out, our bodies are changing all the time anyway. What if this "soul body" or resurrection body simply blossoms at the point of death? After all, our physical bodies have gone through lots of changes throughout the course of our lives. This may simply be the final one. As a seed falls into the ground and dies in order to bring forth the flower, so our bodies fall into the ground and die in order to bring forth the resurrection body. And as the flower grows from the seed, but looks nothing like it, so it may be with our resurrection bodies. They are derived from these mortal bodies, but thrive and are alive with a new kind of life that has grown out of the old.

If the resurrection of Jesus Christ is anything to go by, then this seems to be precisely what does happen. He rose from the dead, but they didn't recognize him at first. In a way, it was like spotting a boy at his college graduation whom you haven't seen for ten or twelve years. You scarcely recognize him, and yet you know the handsome, proud twenty-one-year-old is the same person as the gawky, buck-toothed nine-year-old with a snotty nose. So it will be in our own resurrection. We will have blossomed. We will have grown up to the full maturity of our years. We will be in our prime, and will have reached that potential for which we were created.

Furthermore, there are hints that this bodily resurrection is not just for us, but for the whole world. In a fascinating detail, St. Paul says the whole world "groans for redemption." Like a woman giving birth or like a person groaning in his final agony, the whole of creation is longing for this same resurrection. He seems to be saying that the whole physical realm has this same "soul body," and that every mountain and stone and tree, every flower and beast and fish and living thing is also only partially made. That each one is surging forward to some as-yet unrealised potential. Could it be that each and every living thing will also die and be recreated in a more perfect and fulfilled reality?

If this is so, then the whole point of religion is really quite stupendous. Suddenly, it is not a system of rules to create respectable people or maintain order in society. It is not a formula of faith to bolster people's paranoia. It is not a code of ethics or a criterion of taste or a system of liturgy and ritual. It is about nothing less than the conversion of the whole world into a higher dimension of existence. If this is the case, then the job of each and every person on earth is not simply to be religious and go to church, but to live this stupendous truth in every moment of life.

You and I and every living thing were created only to be recreated through the transaction called death. We are put here, along with the whole of creation, to become all that we can be. Suddenly, the wonder of creation is not that God made everything perfect, but that part of this perfection was that everything was not yet perfect. In other words, we were created with *potential*. This is the genius of his creation, that he made it with a built-in system of growth and progress. To be truly perfect beings, we had to have free will. We had to be able to grow and develop and make mistakes and learn from experience. If this is true, then it also begins to answer the riddle of human suffering. We could have been created without suffering, but to be totally perfect we had to go down through the mess of corruption, rebellion, foolishness and horror, and come through the other side. And we could only do this fully by being these strange hybrid creatures of body and soul combined.

When we speak of the resurrection body, therefore, we speak of the soul-body person totally united and completed. This resurrection body is not something other than what we know now, but it is something transformed. Finally, as I have hinted elsewhere, this resurrection body is not less physical than this one, but more so. It is to this poor, sad, broken-down body what a real person is to a pen-and-ink caricature. The drawing is monochrome and flat. The real resurrected person is in three-dimensional color. He lives and moves and laughs with uproarious joy. He is once and for all time, abundantly, unimaginably and everlastingly alive.

CHAPTER NINETEEN

Eternity in a Grain of Sand

...and the life everlasting...

T HE CHILD IN Sunday School who hears about "eternal life" will think that it is simply life that goes on and on and on and on...and on and on and on. Those with a bit more imagination will conclude that this sort of life would certainly have quantity, but may lack quality. "What on earth are you going to *do* forever and ever and ever?"

The answer is that you're not going to do anything on earth; you're going to do things in heaven. And lest you think that "heaven" is a place beyond the clouds where cherubs sing and willowy, androgynous blondes play harps, "heaven" is the place in another dimension in which all things good and beautiful and true have their source and find their fulfillment.

That's what the concept of "everlasting life" opens up. In other words, just as the idea of something being "everlasting" is unimaginable, so "life everlasting" is another unthinkable kind of life in another, ineffable realm. It's a form of life that we cannot hope to ken, because it has none of the physical and metaphysical constraints that we take for granted, and which make our life normal and liveable.

Here we are constrained by the physical properties of place and time. We have bodies that have to be in one place, and we experience time as a sequence of moments from beginning to end. "Everlasting life" breaks out of those boundaries. It is an invitation, therefore, to the very edge of reality.

Brushes with this frontier are the stuff of near-death experiences. Some people have begun the final adventure. They've taken the first few steps and then returned. They've got a glimpse of the other side and but were sent back to tell their story. For my money, let others explore outer space. I think this inner space is far more exciting and thrilling and disturbing. Here humanity reaches into the realm of eternity and encounters a new kind of life and a new dimension of reality that, I am certain, is not only real, but far more fearful and beautiful than any artist could imagine.

Science fiction stories are fascinating because they often play games with time. Time machines, time warps and time slips are all part of their elastic world. The other thing science fiction bounces around is the idea of space. Science fiction characters zip from place to place and from one world to another like the man on the flying trapeze.

I like the rubberiness of space and time in science fiction because Christianity has a similarly elastic attitude. Somehow, I've never really understood most people's awestruck feelings when confronted by the vast distances of outer space. In science we were taught about light years and parsecs and how planetary systems and galaxies were eons away, and it was all done in an atmosphere of hushed, religious whispers. Even if the distances were vast, I didn't understand why one ought to be amazed simply because something was big. Size isn't necessarily an indication of value. A half-acre in Manhattan is worth more (monetarily) than ten thousand acres in Mississippi. Neither is size a sign of superiority. We don't consider an elephant more important than an infant.

I remember as a teenager suspecting that the whole size-of-the-universe thing was a diversion to take our minds away from the essential issue—rather as the magician grabs your attention with his right hand to pull off his trick with the left. The reason it seemed like an illusion was because it was reliant on the presumed stability of time. When you stop to think about it, distance is not really the measurement of miles or kilometers or inches or feet. Distance is simply the amount of time it takes us to get from one place to another.

If distance is really not a measurement of space, but a measurement of time, then space is time and time is space. What I mean is that if distance is really only the amount of time it takes to get somewhere, then if there were no such thing as time, then there would also be no such thing as distance. So the vast cosmos which we perceive, with its endless array of galaxies and its limitless expanse of neverending star systems may not be vast at all. If time should be suspended, then it would all shrink down to a very cozy size. It may, in fact, be vast, but then again, it may be as small as a single cell.

If you take away time, then there is no distance between objects, and that means you would be everywhere at once. If you are everywhere at once, then you would also be in every time at once. If the sequence of time dissolved, then anything alive would exist in an everlasting single moment in which all events and all places existed in a suspended, yet dynamic unity.

There is a problem with this imaginative scenario. If everything exists in one timeless moment, then it sounds dead and still. But if it is alive and active, then it must move and change, and as soon as something changes or moves it creates time, because there is then a sequence of events. What if, however, the everlasting moment is somehow both at rest and in action at the same time? The one human activity where this seems to happen is in one of those courtly dances that we see in costume dramas from the eighteenth century. In such dances, everyone moves in a set pattern in a single action with one another and with the music. They are in constant harmonious motion and yet, in a way, they are at rest. All of this leads me to suspect that the "life everlasting," or what we call heaven, may be very like an eighteenth-century ball.

Maybe this is why the theologian Karl Barth was convinced that the music of Mozart was the music of heaven. It may be, but I doubt whether we will all wear satin breeches and white powdered wigs. I doubt whether the ladies in heaven will have fans, feathers in their hair and revealing décolletage. No. Instead, the figure of a ball, or a courtly dance is the figure of the life everlasting because it is the earthly image that means the most when we try to imagine what the life everlasting could possibly be like.

Most of all, the life everlasting is characterized by the fact that we will be outside of time. This sounds improbable to those of us who can only imagine life as something bound by time. But what if there really were such a thing as a timeless existence? Furthermore, don't you get the impression that time is somehow provisional or temporary? Haven't you often felt that living in time, you are somehow breathing an alien atmosphere? Don't you suspect that you were made for another kind of existence? An existence outside of time? Why else would you be so constantly surprised by time? Consider the evidence. You travel to visit your brother, and your nephew comes into the room. You haven't seen him for two years and you gasp, "Freddie! You've grown! I hardly recognized you!" Why should you be surprised by Freddie's growth unless you were surprised by time?

Similarly, haven't you felt most alive and most real in those precious and rare moments when time seems suspended and you step outside your time consciousness for a moment? This seems to happen it two ways, one mundane and one extraordinary. We often step outside our awareness of time when we are absorbed in some particular job or pastime that we enjoy. We are transported outside ourselves and we suddenly glance at the watch and are amazed at how time has "flown by." Once again, this is everyday evidence that time is not natural for us, and we are constantly surprised and irritated by both its fleetness and its length.

The other example is those extraordinary moments when we are taken outside time by some sudden experience of beauty, tragedy, truth or joy. It may be as simple as a dust-filled shaft of sunlight on an autumn afternoon. It may be the laughter of a child, the tears of an old widow, or the curves in a Renaissance painting. It may be the hilarity of the circus, the thrill of a gripping story or an exalted moment of love. In these moments of enlightenment, we are lifted beyond time into the timeless moment and so glimpse the very fringe of immortality.

When we say that we believe in the life everlasting, we are affirming with belief our suspicion that there is a timeless existence, and that this is the sort of existence we were made for. We were designed for joy unspeakable and full of glory. We were created to live in that timeless moment when our self-consciousness fades and we can not only be real, but really integrated into our unique place in the intricate and simple dance of the whole creation. This life everlasting is the life of eternity, but it is not meant to be enjoyed only in the afterlife.

Too often we imagine that this everlasting life is reserved for after death. We imagine that it is the reward. But the experience of the children, the poets and the saints tells us that this kind of life is actually available here and now. If everlasting life is one timeless moment, then this moment right now is also life everlasting. For those who can see it, time itself (like space) is an illusion. To stand things on their head, we can ask whether there is any reality at all in time as it is popularly conceived. Does the past exist, except in fond memories, feelings of regret, newspaper clippings and archived film? Does the future exist, except in imagination, anticipation, fear, and science fiction? Both past and future are ethereal and unreal. But this present moment is alive and real. This present moment is just as eternal as the most everlasting life imaginable in heaven.

The saints are those people who have learned how to live each moment of life as if it is a little forever, and because they can do this, they live in heaven now. William Blake sang the same tune. He saw eternity in a grain of sand and said, "He who bends himself a joy/ Does the winged life destroy/ But he who kisses the joy as it flies/ lives in eternity's sunrise." In other words, to live in that moment of perpetual flight and perpetual stillness is to live on the very edge of eternity right here and right now in this very moment. In contrast, to live in the constant fear of the future or the anger and regret of the past is to make for ourselves a kind of living hell.

Instead of looking back with regret and forward with fear, one of the gifts of life everlasting will be to view the whole of life in a single instant. Then we will look on this life not as a series of random decisions or a series of mistakes and successes. Instead our whole life, indeed the whole of life, will appear as it really is: an intricate and seamless tapestry in which every bad choice was only a necessary dark thread in the whole picture. Then we will see that the mistakes have been the side steps in the dance. The wrong turnings will have become the scenic route, and even the most terrible and shameful actions will turn out to be just another step in the long journey home.

Heaven may be represented by a dance, but the burning life of heaven and the still and silent beauty of eternity are also symbolized by the fire and the rose. The heavenly fire of Heraclitus glows like the burning bush, always aflame, but never consumed. Everlasting life burns in a constant dynamic heart of flame, always alive and constantly changing, yet never extinguished and never diminished. Along with the constantly burning flame, the visionary (such as Dante) sees the mystic rose. The rose, complex and interleaved, exists in an eternal calm repose. The rose, fragrant and beautiful, exists as the eternal sign of the mystery, beauty, complexity and simplicity at heaven's heart.

Here in this moment, and then in the moment that is every moment, the saint is the one who holds both the fire and the rose and embraces them to her heart. To exist in the everlasting moment, the saints, the poets and the children live in a condition of complete simplicity and trust, "costing not less than everything" (Eliot). They trust because they know, and what they know is this: all shall be well, because all things work together for good to those who love God and who are called according to his purpose. They have seen into the heart of darkness and know that a still, small fire burns there with an eternal intensity. They have seen and know beyond all doubt that, in the words of Julian of Norwich (via T.S. Eliot), "all shall be well and/ All manner of thing shall be well/ When the tongues of flame are in-folded/ Into the crowned knot of fire/ And the fire and the rose are one."

CHAPTER TWENTY

Let It Be

...Amen.

I N MY BEGINNING IS my end and in my end is my beginning, as T.S. Eliot wrote. I know that the beginning of
my life was when two cells met in a cataclysm of delight.
I trust that my end will be a similar explosion of pleasure
and light and that I will enter into the light eternal and
the grace that powers the planets and moves the stars.

If I want to have that end, then each step must lead
me toward that end and every choice and every action
matters. Could it be that what I actually believe will
affect my eternal destiny? Do the thoughts of my head
and the convictions of my heart really matter so much?
It must be so, for the thoughts of my head and the convictions of my heart are what enlighten my decisions
and motivate my actions and therefore determine my
destiny.

In addition to the thoughts of my head and the convictions of my heart I have a will that must be engaged. So often when I think of the will, I think only of "willpower," that strange, losing struggle to lose weight, curb my ego, and conquer lust or laziness. This is only small-time "willpower." A true engagement of the will involves activating the source of our desire. In other words, to engage the will, we must find the passion behind the need for self control. In other words, to change and engage the will, I must learn to find disgusting things disgusting and not delightful. I must begin to genuinely desire (not just desire to desire) what is good and beautiful and true and everlasting. Then the will is truly engaged, and all things are possible.

This transformation of character can only take place through the gift of grace, and that grace is accessed through the chemistry of prayer and contemplation. There must be a stillness of heart and an attentiveness of mind, and in that still point of the turning world, something eternal is seen—and the everlasting is understood.

One day twenty years ago, in the Oriental section of the Victoria and Albert Museum I discovered a pale green Chinese vase. The small vase is ancient, beautiful and frail. It stands with a few other pieces of china in a simple glass cabinet. I stopped for a moment and suddenly realized why someone would pay millions of dollars for such a treasure. As I stood before this vase, I was captivated by its fragile, luminescent beauty. Somehow it cut across the barriers of time to carry the entire majesty of a Chinese dynasty, the mystery of a bygone age, and the integral history of a foreign world. In its exquisite simplicity it seemed to encapsulate the refined mind and manicured hands of its aristocratic owner, as well as the simple mind and soiled hands of the potter who made it. In that moment I sensed a beauty, truth and simplicity which were beyond words, so I quietly said the only word that applied: "Amen."

"Amen" is simply a word of affirmation. It means "so be it" or "let it be." It means, "This is good and great and wonderful beyond all my ideas and words, and I am struck into silence." It means, "This one thing of beauty and truth before me carries all things, and I stand before it as I stand beneath the sky at night, filled with mute wonder and humble gratitude at the magnificence, beauty and order of it all." This was my attitude before the ancient Chinese vase. This is my attitude before the beloved. This is also my attitude at the end of the creed. At this point the dogma takes me beyond dogma, and the words take me beyond words. This is the goal of worship: to take us beyond the blank words to tremble on the precipice of silence.

The creed points us beyond the creed, as the vase pointed beyond itself to an entire other culture. Like the vase, the creed is essentially a simple, everyday useful thing. Its simplicity is in its usefulness. Its eloquence is in its hard, practical language. The clue is not to look too much at the creed, but to look through it to contemplate the vast panorama of truth. Those who dislike creeds point out that the particularity of creeds divide. This is true, but creeds become divisive only when people start to argue about them. When the creed is under attack, believers feel obliged to defend the form of words from erosion and final destruction. Sadly, this exercise often results in minute arguments and overly literal theological discussions, and these discussions often lead to further theological definitions that are intended to defend the simple belief but typically only foster more divisions.

But have you seen what has caused the division? It was not the creed, but its denial. If Christians were simply to affirm the creed and not deny, then the further definitions would not be necessary. In other words, if believers could only say a full and hearty "Amen: let it be," then we all could just let it be. The simple, monumental statements could stand, and the creed would then be a focus for unity, not a source of division. This does not mean we'd never question, but that our questions would be a passionate desire to know more of the mystery, not less. The creed provides a starting point for further discovery. It is a ladder with which to climb, and all real inquiry should be taking us further up the ladder. A spirit of denial, on the other hand, forgets all that and constantly examines the ladder itself and questions whether or not it is strong enough, or whether it is really a ladder at all.

The curious thing is that the very ones who seek to destroy the ladder will blame the ladder's defenders for being divisive. Look at it this way, those who were climbing the ladder were taking it for granted, and using it for its rightful purpose. Then when they discovered someone lower down was sawing away at the rungs, the climbers realized not only that they might fall, but that the ladder would not be intact for those who wished to follow. Then imagine their frustration when they come down to repair the ladder, only to find that they are being blamed for being argumentative, divisive and ladder-obsessed.

Unfortunately, all this theological fuss obscures the point of the creed. The creed is not the whole story. It was never meant to be. It is merely a precis or a summary. It is far from the final word. In fact, it is the first. It is a baby step on the journey, not the terminus. The journey is conducted in a whole range of ways—not just theological reflection. Indeed, for most people, theological reflection scarcely comes into it. Instead, about the creed they say, "Let it be," and the creed becomes a kind of foundation on which the rest of their religious life is built. On its own, the creed is simply a collection of theological words. But integrated into a regular religious life, the creed becomes a kind of support system. So whether we are visiting the sick, campaigning for justice, worshiping at church, praying or singing or studying, every religious action is upheld by the creed, and through all these actions we are living out the creed. Furthermore, for the person of faith, the formal belief supports and enables his whole life, so whether he eats or drinks or laughs or cries; whether he sleeps, works, thinks or has a meal with friends, he is doing it all for the glory of God. Then as we live the Christian life, the words of that ancient formula work their way into our mind and heart and body. As they are acted out, the ideas transform the way we think, the way we see the world and the way we see ourselves and the way we behave.

The creed, like the Chinese vase, is a practical thing. It works. But it is also a thing of beauty, not only because it is simple and integrated, but because it points us to a beauty beyond itself. Quite simply, the creed provides a perspective. It gives us a mountaintop on which to stand, and from that summit we can breathe a clearer air and hear the strains of faraway music. On that peak, the storms may rage, but now and again, as the sun breaks through we can catch a glimpse of that distant land we know is home. Then, if we are lucky, beyond the hills, in a brief moment, the light blazes down to reveal a scrap of the everlasting sea. This is where the creed should bring us—not to theological dead ends, but to a world that never ends. Not to dull intellectual statements, but to the glory of the Father, and the Son and the Holy Spirit. Not to a world that is closed and dying, but to a world that moves in ever-increasing spirals of glory, as it was in the beginning, is now and ever shall be. World without end. World without end. World without end. AMEN.

Acknowledgements

I WISH TO THANK Michael Craft, Bob Trexler and Cyprian Blamires for reading the first edition manuscript of this book and offering their advice and criticisms.

Dom Sebastian Moore OSB, and Fr John Saward helped listen to ideas and refine them while Joseph Pearce and Tom Howard offered sprightly words of encouragement. Todd Aglialoro edited the first time around and John Zmirak helped tighten things up and create a new look and a new cover for a new approach in the second edition.

I also thank my children, Benedict, Madeleine, Theodore and Elias for helping to keep me sane and my wife Alison for her loving support and for being willing to go on an adventure or two with me over the years.

Related Reading

GOD AT THE RITZ
Attraction to Infinity
Lorenzo Albacete
ISBN 978-0-8245-2472-2

New York Times columnist Lorenzo Albacete shares his thoughts on religion and God—and why they both still matter.

With great humor and intellect, *God at the Ritz* offers another way forward. From Charlie Rose and the God Squad to the pages of the Sunday *New York Times* magazine, Lorenzo Albacete is a leading voice on the power of religion in American life. In the national bestselling and critically acclaimed God at the Ritz, Albacete, a physicist and Catholic priest, offers profound, honest, and entertaining insights into the power of religion for good and evil and the need for religion at the core of human existence.

"Lorenzo Albacete is one of a kind, and so is *God at the Ritz*. The book, like the monsignor, crackles with humor, warmth, and intellectual excitement. Reading it is like having a stay-up-all-night, jump-out-of-your-chair, have-another-espresso marathon conversation with one of the world's most swashbuckling talkers." – Hendrik Hertzberg, *The New Yorker*

Support your local bookstore or order
directly from the publisher by calling
1-800-888-4741 for customer service.

To request a catalog or inquire about
Quantity orders, please e-mail
info@CrossroadPublishing.com

The Crossroad Publishing Company

ONE

From Bulls to Chickens

ONE OF THE NICE THINGS about flying on the air shuttle back and forth between New York City and Washington, D.C., is that you can stay up to date about when human beings first appeared on the earth. It's all there in those magazines and journals you find at the air shuttle terminals — you know, those low-circulation brain stimulators with extraordinary titles like *Intelligence, Insanity, Discrimination, Weather in Siberia, Rocks and Precipices,* and the *Journal of Prehistoric Studies.* Sooner or later one of these has an article about the age of humankind. But you really need to keep up with this information, because it keeps changing.

The stories always talk about those caves that explorers keep finding. They contain evidence of prehistoric human dwellings, and when archaeologists date the artifacts in them, they keep pushing back the date of the first humans, usually by millions of years! So don't bother memorizing the date, because eventually another cave will turn up and move the date even further back. But you can keep up with it pretty well by flying the air shuttle and grabbing all the magazines you can.

I can't help but wonder, though, who keeps finding these caves. You'd think that by now a scientific society somewhere would just go on an intense search for all of them and put the whole matter to rest. But most of the time, the people who find them aren't even looking for them. Shepherd boys, for example, seem to have a special knack for finding caves with wonderful manuscripts in them — manuscripts containing texts from documents that everyone thought were written hundreds of years later.

To the untrained eye, all these caves look the same. You'd almost think these arcane magazines keep reusing the same photos. The manuscripts, tools, artifacts, pottery, and, of course, bones, all look absolutely identical to the untrained eye. The most stunning feature in those caves, however, is this huge jumping (or is it flying?) bull-type creature pictured on the cave wall. It's always there, and no matter where the cave is, the bull is always surrounded by some incomprehensible prehistoric graffiti. No matter how much farther back in time the new cave allows us to peer, no matter where the cave is found — the bull is always there.

Now here's the amazing thing: according to the archaeologists, this bull is an example of prehistoric religious art. The bull is a religious symbol of sorts. It's evidence of the religious preoccupations of prehistoric people — evidence of their religious sense, their spiritual sensitivities, their perception of mystery. Okay, maybe so, but the *same* bull? I mean, whoever drew the original bull should probably be hailed as the greatest religious leader of all times, with an influence lasting millions and millions of years. One thing is certain: the evidence for religious pluralism in prehistoric times is pretty slim indeed. The bull reigned supreme, it seems.

I know these are not very scientific thoughts. It's the kind of philosophical musing with which you distract yourself when you're stuck in the middle seat of the air shuttle, wedged in by the dozens of heavy magazines and journals you greedily took at the terminal. It makes you think of dumb jokes like this: in prehistoric times you'd be considered a mystic if you said that religion certainly was a lot of bull.

Still, the persistence of the religious impulse, or longing for God, is truly amazing. Indeed, airports are a good place to confirm this. Airport bookstores today are packed with all kinds of books about religion, the spiritual life, the unknown — the mystery beyond words. If some catastrophe befalls us and destroys civilization "as we know it," shepherd boys of the future will find buried airport terminals and archaeologists will claim they were centers of spirituality, based not on bulls but on *chickens*.

I have in mind, of course, those *Chicken Soup for the Soul* books. I've seen entire shelves dedicated to the famous Chicken Soup series. There's chicken soup for nearly everyone — the cat and dog lover's soul, the unsinkable soul, the golden soul, and most intriguingly chicken soup for the butt. The series seems to be for our age what the *Imitation of Christ* was for the Middle Ages. I confess I haven't read any of these Chicken Soup books, so for all I know they are truly mystical fare, but their popularity is like that of the Dummies series, which started with how-to manuals for computers and now puts out books covering almost everything imaginable, including *aromatherapy* and *feng shui*.

I wonder what Friedrich Nietzsche might have thought of all of this. Back in 1882 he announced that God had died. Maybe God did not die completely but was merely undergoing a metamorphosis — from bull to chicken. That may be the religious saga of humankind. If that is so, then our notion of God has certainly been diminished.

But maybe it's not God who became a chicken — maybe it's us humans. Flannery O'Connor observed that ours had become a generation of "wingless chickens." Apparently if you cut the wings off chickens while they're still alive, the meat gets fatter and more tender, and the chicken tastes better. Unfortunately, the poor chickens, though more desirable, lose the capacity to hop up and down. Not that they were ever soaring eagles, but at least they could jump; they could tell up from down. The wingless chickens cannot. Their world is two-dimensional, like those mathematical figures in Edwin A. Abbott's classic *Flatland*.

So it is with us, according to O'Connor. We certainly have more possessions and knowledge today — we may be existentially fatter — but we have lost an entire dimension of existence. We cannot hop up and down anymore. In fact, we've even lost the sense of what up and down mean. We can only descend to the most primitive psychological levels and ascend to our most exalted view of material progress.

But the religious experience is much more than that. It originates on a level deeper than the psychological, and it takes us beyond all imaginable limits — to infinity. We have lost the capacity to experience this range of possibilities. Not that all of us were soaring eagles like the mystics, but at least we could hop a little. We could hop up and move toward the infinity of the Holy, or hop down into the depths of the Holy. But now we no longer know how to hop up and down. We are wingless chickens.

The religious impulse, however — the desire to hop up and down, or, in more "religious" language, to long for an encounter with the Holy — remains as powerful as ever. It is, shall we say, as strong as a bull. Perhaps that's why, so many centuries ago, our ancestors painted those captivating and powerful images of bulls on the walls of torch-lit caves. Perhaps that's why we look in airport bookstores for *Chicken Soup* and other books that will feed our spiritual hunger. We long for God.